£1060

ATLANTIC ODYSSEY

ATLANTIC ODYSSEY

MICHAEL THWAITES

NEW CHERWELL PRESS · OXFORD

First published in Great Britain 1999
by New Cherwell Press
7 Mount Street, Oxford OX2 6DH
Copyright © Michael Thwaites 1999
Second impression 1999

ISBN 1 900312 30 1 (hbk)
ISBN 1 900312 35 2 (pbk)

Cover illustration by Robert Thwaites
Cover design by Philip Carr
Printed by Biddles, Guildford

CONTENTS

PREFACE

This is a true story from the Battle of the Atlantic, the only battle which lasted from the first day of World War Two until the German surrender on 8 May 1945, the only battle where Churchill feared a German victory.

War clouds were gathering over Europe when I, and then my best-beloved, came to Britain from Australia. The war years saw our marriage, the loss of our first child, the birth of our eldest son and our daughter. They included my six years' Naval service in trawlers and corvettes, in the Atlantic and the North Sea; and, for my wife, the life of a wartime housewife and mother, with her parents and family on the other side of the world, and husband away at sea.

Not for one moment did either of us doubt the choice we had made to stay in Britain. Not for a moment did we question the necessity of defeating Hitler at all and any cost, for the future not just of Britain and Australia but of the whole world. Unlike so many millions we survived and came through unscathed.

Those years brought the gift of friendships which have proved lifelong, and experiences beyond all price.

In particular I thank Britain for admitting me to two of her greatest educational institutions: Oxford University and the Royal Navy.

Michael Thwaites
April 1999

ACKNOWLEDGEMENTS

I am extremely grateful to those who have read my manuscript and encouraged publication, including Lord and Lady Bullock, Sir Anthony Kenny, Warden of Rhodes House, Peter Ryan, Anne Edgeworth, loyal family members, and an array of friends, including Nada Bond and Carol Russell, who typed the manuscript, John Bond, Dorothy Rogers, John Williams, Jim Coulter, Chris Mayor, Bill and Margo Stallybrass, Robin Mowat, A.R.K. Mackenzie, Ken and Beryl Mackay, Charis Waddy, Douglas Allen, Neville Haile, John Farquharson, June Wallace.

I have particularly appreciated the enthusiastic support of Jack Wilson of New Zealand, friend and shipmate in *Wastwater*, who supplied many of the photographs.

The *Tale of the Ferry Boat That Met a U-Boat* was first printed in *Newsweek* on 21 October 1942.

My sincere thanks to Professor Robert O'Neill, Chichele Professor of the History of War, All Souls College, Oxford, for his interest and encouragement.

CHAPTER 1

A SUMMER'S IDYLL

My training course at HMS *King Alfred,* a converted underground car-park at Hove, Sussex, came to an end. King Alfred's motto, "making bricks without straw", was apt. Six weeks had not been an extravagant period for the transforming of an inexperienced, academically-inclined landsman, however keen, into a naval officer, however junior. But the needs were urgent, and the next course was waiting.

"Here's your travel warrant. Your train for Glasgow leaves King's Cross at nineteen fifty." This, my first posting, was to the "stone frigate", HMS *Fortitude,* the naval base at the small port and seaside resort of Ardrossan on the Clyde. A phone call brought Honor, my beloved of five years and wife of six weeks, from her London office in time to see me off at King's Cross; after that I settled back in my First Class compartment, wrapped in my long naval greatcoat. As the night-train groped its way across a blacked-out countryside and through snow-capped, moonlit hills, M.R. Thwaites, Temporary Probationary Acting Sub-Lieutenant, Royal Naval Volunteer Reserve, prepared for his first day of active service against Hitler's monstrous tyranny.

I presented myself to the Naval Officer-in-Charge, Commander Waite. "Who are you?" I showed my papers. "Trawler group — why the hell don't they tell us? Report to the Group Commander. He's at sea — back tomorrow."

I was given a seat in the cypher office, where demure Wrens were busy coding and decoding signals under the eye of a bombastic Captain of Marines. The real oracle was the Chief Yeoman of Signals, a small, sharp Cockney, who knew everything. I did not get the impression that anyone had been anxiously awaiting my arrival.

My appointment was Liaison Officer to a group of five trawlers which carried out anti-submarine patrols in the vital Clyde estuary, the gateway to the North Atlantic convoy routes. Every third night I was required to be night duty officer at the base, sleeping on a stretcher by the telephone, with a loaded revolver. I had never fired a shot in anger, so was happy not to be called upon to repel any boarding parties. Ignorance was my standby. An urgent voice would say: "Duty officer? Look, you know we've got some big chaps coming in tonight?"

"No, Sir, sorry."

"Good Lord, hasn't Waite told you? Put me through to him."

Waite's peace-time job had been floor manager in a big London store. He liked to keep every string in his own hands. One night there was real excitement. One of our sloops had sunk a U-boat, and a clutch of captured documents was hurried through our base with the utmost secrecy on their way to the Admiralty. Only much later did I realise how vital to the whole war at sea such windfalls could be.

I soon began to grasp that I was unlikely either to win or to lose the war single-handed. A brother officer, observing my tendency to anxiety, offered some kindly advice. "Always be seen going somewhere with a piece of paper in your hand and you'll be all right."

At *King Alfred* we had been drilled in carrying respirators as an essential part of uniform, and in punctilious saluting. At the trawler base, staffed largely by ex-fishermen and civilians, saluting was perfunctory and cumbersome respirators were dumped.

My first responsibility was to look after the interests of the five ships in our group, ensuring a flow of cigarettes, stores and information from the base. I was also to go out on patrols, to learn the rudiments of seafaring and naval life. My boyhood fascination with ships and the sea had suddenly become my life and calling. I revelled in it.

Britain at that point was gripped by an extraordinary sense of common purpose and challenge. Strangers talked to each other in trains. Barriers came down. Confidences were shared. A fellow officer at the base confided in me, seeking counsel. His problem was not global. He had a fiancée whom he held in high regard and considered marrying. But he also had a car for which he had a similar high regard. He could not afford both: which should he choose? I listened sympathetically, but did not feel I could advise him. I had never had a car, anyway.

Soon I had someone to talk to. Honor handed over her job in the Germany Emergency Committee to her friend Marga, and came north to join me. We found lodgings at 1 Burnfoot, easy walking distance from the base. It was a tall red stone house and was the home of a widow, Christina Gilfillen, "Tinny" to her friends. She came to the door when I knocked. I asked the rent. Lifting her eyes shyly she enquired, "Would twenty-three shillings a week be too much?" As a married man, my Sub-Lieutenant's nine shillings a day had been boosted to fourteen shillings. We took it. We had a small upstairs bedroom, a downstairs sitting room with dining table, windows looking across the Clyde to the mountains of Arran, and use of bathroom and kitchen. It was an unbelievable gift, a haven together instead of the separation we had expected. We hired a piano and Honor played Bach to her heart's content.

We had friends and brother officers in to meals, walked in the lovely Ayrshire hills, and came back to our own hearth and home. After a cold, snow-bound winter came a late but lavish spring. For both of us that spring, though not our first in the northern hemisphere, was by far our most stunning and dramatic, as dead earth and dry sticks suddenly exploded into life. With naval analogies I wrote a poem.

The Tactician

Spring held her fire
So long, the long pursuit, the watchers wondered
Would there be ever an end, would Winter's keel
Plough the grey lifeless land without a challenge,
Hated but all too strong, and the earth beaten
This year, and bud and blossom bound too fast?
But Spring, the tactician, came,
Certain of herself, silently closing in
On the confident foe. Now, surely, and now

3

Is the minute of destiny. Strike, nor lose it! Still
Never a shot, and the minute passing. And now
Too late, perhaps, and the battle lost.

                         She touched
In hedge and tree and lane the explosive charge,
And with one broadside sank the enemy Winter
Under the green wave.

These were the months of the "phoney war". After the shock of the Hitler-Stalin pact, Britain's declaration of war, the swift defeat and partition of Poland, the overrunning of Denmark and occupation of Norway, there followed a deceptive calm. The French and British forces consolidated behind the Maginot Line, while Churchill's government struggled to re-arm after the years the locusts had eaten, and to strengthen British morale. In fact, though we did not know it, Hitler still hoped to do a deal which would keep Britain out of the war.

Meanwhile, as I grappled with my new naval duties, Honor for the first time confronted the responsibilities of housekeeping. "It was a shock," she recalled, "to realize that I, who had perhaps boiled an egg once a week when the maid was out, had to provide our total nourishment — twenty-one meals a week!" When she ventured on her first cake, Tinny helped, and hovered. When it was time to open the oven door, Tinny said, "I'll just leave you for a wee while," and disappeared. All was well.

I hated underdone meat. When Honor's first roast was laid on the table and I began to carve, a thin red trickle ran out and I made a face. Our marriage survived: precariously.

The news from Europe of Fifth Columnists in Holland and Quislings in Norway spread fear in Britain of spies and parachutists. A road-block was placed twenty yards from 1 Burnfoot, with a youthful sentry (LDV, "Local Defence Volunteer", until Churchill insisted on "Home Guard"). Returning from shopping, Honor was stopped. She had left her Identity Card at home. Her distress prevailed. The young sentry looked away and let her through with the words, "Och, it's immaterial".

Air Raid Wardens patrolled, to ensure effective blackouts of all lighted windows. Honor pointed out to Tinny that her roof skylight was quite uncovered. "It's no matter," said Tinny. "The Air Raid Warden will never see it."

But Nemesis followed a few nights later. A real German plane, presumably on reconnaissance, flew over. As the sirens howled, Honor and Tinny hid under the stairs. (I was on duty at the base.) Tinny was in abject penitence and contrition. The plane was high and dropped no bombs. However, in a panic, one of our trawlers let fly with its Lewis gun and shot away a corner of its own bridge.

The five trawlers of "Group Twenty-Nine" had been built for deep-sea fishing. They could stay at sea for three weeks and travel as far as Spain, Greenland or the White Sea. They symbolised Britain's hasty transition from peace to war. They were still painted their commercial colours, green hulls, buff upperworks, red funnels; but they had been converted for anti-submarine work, with depth charges, a four-inch gun, Lewis guns and a machine gun, as well as the submarine detection device Asdic. They were *Lord Essendon* (flagship), *Lord Austin, Lord Middleton, Lord Nuffield* and (the only commoner), *Lincolnshire.* Each had a Skipper, a Coxswain, a Gunner, a "Chief" (engineman) and fourteen deck and engine-room hands.

For me it was an introduction to areas of life in pre-war Britain that I would never have encountered in peace-time. The trawler skippers had handled their vessels and crews over years of peace-time fishing. In harbour, over drinks in the wardroom, they would relax and exchange stories which held me fascinated. Their spontaneous eloquence, colour, drama and humour were a revelation. They reflected the uninhibited debate in wardroom and mess deck which seafaring life, perhaps especially in war-time, made possible

Senior to the skippers were two Lieutenants with experience in the peace-time RNVR: Butcher, a shrewd business executive, and Buckley, a genial hospital administrator and devout Catholic.

They became friends and allies, and we soon discovered that they were a vital stabilising element, essential to the orderly functioning of Group Twenty-Nine.

The Group Commander (the "GC"), Lieutenant Commander Nichol-Cadell RN (straight stripes) was certainly one of the most flamboyant and unforgettable characters I ever met, in the Navy or out of it. He was the cause of the note which I made in a diary as I began to understand the situation: "Group Twenty-Nine is already famous at the Base. We have caused more trouble and annoyance than all the other ships put together; we have alienated the hearts of a good proportion of the older and more senior officers of HMS *Fortitude*; but at least we have avoided mediocrity; we have not passed unnoticed."

Later I wrote of the GC: "Whether to be laughed at, cursed, admired or deprecated, he has succeeded in making himself a leader whom it is impossible not to talk about".

He was colourful by nature and cultivation, with flaming red hair and tanned, worn features. He warmly welcomed me as his "Sub", invited Honor and me to dine aboard *Essendon*, visited and came for walks with us behind Ardrossan.

Aspects of his story emerged. From an upper-class Irish Catholic family he was educated at a Jesuit school in England and at Dartmouth Naval College; served in World War I, from Midshipman to Lieutenant, and with peace was discharged under the "Geddes Axe". Thereafter came Cambridge and half an English Tripos. When he heard that I had won the Newdigate Prize at Oxford, his eyes flashed and he declaimed from his favourite poet, Willie Yeats:

> I saw a staring virgin stand
> Where holy Dionysus died ...

Honor was startled. Her family background had not brought many characters like him into her orbit. He was in many ways a child of the 1920s and the D.H. Lawrence era. The inter-war years took him to Ceylon, where he had acquired a bungalow, a native fishing boat and a charming-looking Ceylonese wife. He never spoke of her, but his cabin was covered with photographs of her, smiling, wistful, in European bridal dress, holding a dog or, in a sari, standing beside him in his ferocious beachcomber's apparel, his fiery red hair tossed into a mop by the wind. No doubt in the arrogant but common parlance of that era, many of his English contemporaries would have considered that he had "gone native".

Whatever the past, the war and his recall to the colours as a Lieutenant Commander had opened the door to a role which he relished to the full. As Commander of Trawler Group Twenty-Nine, he saw himself as supremo of his own fleet, with more than a dash of Nelson and Admiral Beatty.

He either had considerable means, or pretended to have them, spending freely on himself and others. In fact *Essendon*'s skipper, James Denoon, a canny and careful Scot, took me aside and whispered anxiously, "He doesna' ken the varlue o' money!" Along with the imperious air of one born to command, he was easy-going, informal, humane, even indulgent. He got great amusement from his personal steward, Noble, a raw Scot who had unexpected gifts as a water-colour artist (I have one of his highly competent pictures of a trawler travelling at full speed). Noble served at table when we went to dinner, as he cleared each glass turning his back and tossing off remainders. Frequently he could be seen seated at the GC's desk sketching, with paint brushes between his teeth or behind his ears.

The GC saw me as an Admiral sees his Flag-Lieutenant. It was "Sub, here!" or "Sub, there — show a leg!" or "Come on, Sub, we'll go up to Base and tackle that bloody Paymaster," when I would be drawn unwillingly into his latest skirmish.

He used all of everything. The worried manager of the South Beach Hotel, where the GC had evidently run up an account, took me aside and asked anxiously, "Is he really related to Royalty?" (I had no comment.)

It was the GC's tragedy that his period of command was devoid of enemy action. He had to seek the enemy which his nature required in another quarter. The choice seemed inevitable.

Waite, Naval Officer-in-Charge of *Fortitude*, and the GC's superior, issued an order that trawlers on patrol were not to pass through a narrow passage, the Kyles of Bute. Before long he received a report from the nearest signal station that two trawlers had just passed through. They were the flagship *Lord Essendon*, with the GC, followed by *Lord Austin*. On return to Base, the GC received (as he fully expected), a signal from the NOIC requesting his reasons in writing for disobeying an explicit order. With glee he cleared his desk and set about drafting a reply. Butcher, who was present, described the scene. Courteously and correctly, the GC set out his case. The nub of it was that, as Group Commander, he was responsible for bringing his ships to the highest point of operational efficiency. He considered it essential that his crews should be familiar with all waters, however narrow, where U-boats might penetrate. As a sea-going commander, he believed the judgement on this must be his.

The last point was crucial. Waite had a case; his order had been disregarded. But we were at war. If Waite had taken the issue higher, to the C-in-C ... Butcher laughed. The weight of traditional prejudice could have swung in favour of the sea-going as against the shore-based officer. Waite prudently let the matter drop.

The GC had won the first round. But his real enemy resided in a bottle. I never saw, or heard of, his being under the influence of alcohol at sea. But in the intervals in port it was a different matter, when he lived at the Eglinton Arms hotel, not far from the base. His natural ebullience could be replaced by unpredictable temper and moods of sullen moroseness. It was my routine to report to him at the end of each day before I left for 1 Burnfoot. Some evenings he would be in a testy mood. "No, I don't want you, Sub — Get off home to your wife!" Another evening, he was sombre and imperious: "Come and see me at my hotel after dinner." I duly returned to the Eglinton at 8 pm. He was sitting alone at a small table in the large, gloomy dining room, clearly far gone. When I reported, he turned on me with a bibulous, hostile glare: "What are you here for?" I reminded him of his instruction but he swept me aside. "Bugger off! Bugger off!"

The end was foreseeable. One night, returning to the base cantankerously drunk, he attacked the sentry on duty and disarmed him of his rifle: a Naval sin beyond excuse, manifest to all. We saw the GC no more. Discreetly he was posted away to a battleship, where he would be under the eyes of numerous senior officers heavy with gold braid: for him the worst fate imaginable. Later, I heard on the grapevine that at sea one night he had disappeared over the side. He was a human casualty of two world wars.

For Honor and me the Ardrossan interlude seemed too good to be true. In this totally new setting she found, through the Oxford Group, a range of friends: the Cochrane-Patricks, generous hosts at their lovely country house "Ladylands"; the Hutchisons, with four daughters, in whose Glasgow home she was fascinated to see a whole family exploring together the idea of finding direction from the still, small, inner voice; and in Ardrossan, Mary Hunter, the wife of an industrial plumber, who became a warm friend.

Tinny proved a constant ally. No longer regarding the Air Raid Warden as her main threat, she followed the BBC wireless news with growing concern, murmuring, "They Gairmans, they're gittin' awn, they're gittin' awn".

For us young newly-weds she had a sensitive heart. One morning I arrived back at 1 Burnfoot with an unexpected whole day's leave. Tinny put on her bonnet. "I'm away to my friends," she said. "I'll be away all afternoon."

As we lay in bed in our little upstairs bedroom through the long afternoon, we heard a soft, misty rain falling, like a blessing on our peaceful, complete happiness. The here and now was sufficient in itself. No need to question, or to probe the unpredictable future. We were Babes in the Wood certainly; but within ourselves we had no doubts. Perhaps it was a state of grace. It so, it was a total gift, unexpected, unearned, but cherished.

From our earliest days together we had thought of marrying and having children, and had even spoken of it; but marriage itself seemed then such a far-off prospect. We had no sense that war should change our plans. We had each been given so much and spared so much in our lives that we had an irrational assumption, based on profound inexperience, that if we stepped forward boldly everything would work out. However, when Honor told me that she was pregnant, my delight was mixed with a disconcerting shock as I confronted, but hardly comprehended, the new situation.

That golden summer was hailed by German media as "Hitler weather". The Germans seemed unstoppable. After the rapid conquest and partition of Poland, the defeat of France, which surrendered on 22 June, was accomplished with startling speed. The Dunkirk evacuation and Churchill's rhetoric sustained British morale, but Germany held all Europe.

What sustained us was our passionate belief, shared by almost everyone in embattled Britain, that if Hitler won, there would be no world worth living in for us or any children we might have. When Italy declared war on 10 May, it confirmed my growing feeling that, as a young, fit man of 25, I should request service at sea instead of my sheltered apprenticeship in a shore job.

Honor felt differently, on the basis of "Why meet trouble half way? They'll send for you when they need you". We knew couples who had split up on this issue. But we had committed ourselves to asking direction from a wisdom greater than our own. We got down on our knees. Soon I got up and said, "I think I should go." She said, "I think you should go." She went off and ironed a shirt for me.

We had an unforgettable brief leave on beautiful Arran, in delicious summer weather. Completely ignoring her pregnancy, we hired bicycles and rode round the island. On the last morning we decided we must get to the top of the highest peak, Goatfell. Honor recalls:

> It was one of those absolute jewels of a morning ... When we finally reached the top, after a pretty tough scramble, there was the whole of the West Coast of Scotland — all the

10

isles and mountains and bays looking absolutely like a Disney set; the colours varying from turquoise through to emerald and sapphire ... It was just so breathtaking, and although I never got to the Highlands because they were a restricted area in the war years, I carry that with me always as my picture of the Western Isles.

In idyllic summer weather, warm sun, blue sky, spring leaves in the hedgerows and fields, we listened to Churchill's famous speech of defiance: "We will fight them on the beaches ... We will fight them on the hills ... We will never give up ...".

That was my goodbye to 1 Burnfoot, our cherished haven. From then on, for five and a half years as it turned out, my home would be in ships, and on the fascinating, deadly, unresting ocean.

CHAPTER 2

THE BATTLE OF BRITAIN

My first ship was *Northern Dawn*, a large trawler built in German shipyards as part of reparations to Britain after World War I. She had just come back from the ill-fated British expedition to Narvik, where she had been under bomb attack, but not hit, and was now based at Belfast as an Atlantic convoy escort. I was welcomed by the CO, Lowe, a dapper Lieutenant RNVR, and the genial "Number One", Brian. He had been at Cambridge and was a rowing man; but we agreed that the struggle against Hitler was more important.

My duties included chart-correcting and, at sea, watchkeeping (four hours on, eight hours off). My learning began quickly and painfully. Setting out on my first 500-mile expedition into mid-Atlantic with a convoy of merchant ships, I was given the Dog Watches (4 to 8 pm). Passing the craggy Mull of Kintyre, we steered along the north coast of Ireland with its hills, bays and rugged cliffs. Presently the Captain, who was with me, said, "Well — there you are, Sub. Take over; I'm going below". For the first time ever, I was alone, in charge of the ship as it plunged forward, as though with its own will and purpose. This was not the sheltered Clyde. I checked the course on the compass, paced a few steps up and down, swept the horizon with my binoculars, began to relax. Suddenly crisis struck. A heavy squall of rain came from nowhere; coast and convoy were alike shrouded, invisible; we were alone on the ocean. At that moment Lowe reappeared. "What's happened? Where's the convoy?" I pointed in a general direction. "What was the bearing of the last ship?" I didn't know. "What's our position, course and speed?" I dived into the chart-table to ascertain. At that moment I was ready to believe I had lost the convoy, perhaps also the war.

Lowe was terse but matter-of-fact. I showed him our position. To my huge relief, the squall cleared as quickly as it had come; and there were the tail-end ships of the convoy, plodding in order, unperturbed.

Lesson One. Lesson Two: this time not my fault. Lowe brought unexpected news from the base: we were ordered to proceed immediately to Dartmouth on England's south coast. Secrets of high strategy were not showered on such as us; but our role was clear enough: to counter Hitler's plan (which he had code-named *Sealion*) to achieve what had not been done since the Norman Conquest: the invasion of Britain.

Napoleon had prepared for and then abandoned the same project. With the advent of Churchill as Prime Minister and a reaction among the British people he had not expected, Hitler had postponed his hopes of doing a deal with Britain and had assembled massive forces along the French coast, with a fleet of barges and transports, and had given his service chiefs a provisional invasion date. German documents later revealed growing misgivings among his military and naval chiefs. Goering alone was supremely confident that his Luftwaffe could destroy Britain's air defences, and bring Britain to her knees.

In this crisis we and other trawlers were transferred to the front line. In summer calm we sailed down the Irish Sea, and rounded Land's End. We had passed Lizard Point when I came up for my Middle Watch (midnight to 4 am). Brian, our navigator, said, "There's your course; call me if you need me," and went below. Presently the lookout drew my attention to a looming mass of land in the darkness ahead. I called Brian. He agreed. Maybe we had altered course a little too soon. "Steer out to sea for a couple of miles and get on course again." I obeyed; but unease grew. "Land ahead, Sir," and then, "Channel-marking buoy alongside, Sir." Brian and Lowe appeared simultaneously in alarmed consultation. As day dawned, we saw that we were on our way into the harbour of Fowey, Cornwall. Brian was chagrined and penitent. He had made the classic error in navigating with a magnetic compass, by applying the correction (variation plus deviation) the wrong way. I was excused as a new boy, but imbibed an unforgettable cautionary tale.

The picture-book harbour of Dartmouth was our home during the fateful months of the Battle of Britain, August and September

1940. As we operated only at night, we could snatch hours of leave ashore. In the golden weather which gave Goering his best chance of devastating daylight attacks on RAF bases, factories and the population of London, Brian and I took several walks into the charming Devon hills, stopping at wayside tea-houses to feast on fresh scones with blackberry jam and Devonshire clotted cream.

Our task was night-patrolling of the channel. To deal with the enemy, our armament was our four-inch gun with 60 rounds, Lewis guns and several boxes of Mills bombs (hand-grenades). As far as we could see, naval forces along the south coast were limited to trawlers and a few destroyers. All larger ships were withdrawn far to the north. In the event of an actual invasion, the best we could hope for would be to sell our lives dearly. Night patrols under war-time conditions were nerve-wracking. We were without radar — later such a boon — and cruising in darkness in narrow waters without navigation-lights produced the mishap which ships' captains dreaded more than enemy action: collision. It was with another trawler and damage was fortunately minimal. But among merchant ships at the beginning of the war, losses by collision were as serious as losses by enemy action.

We did not encounter enemy shipping and were not on the main bomber routes. But we did see from time to time, high in the blue, the vapour trails of combat aircraft; and we knew well that our fate, and that of Britain, depended on the outcome. Each evening we sat glued to the BBC 6 o'clock wireless news.

On 15 August the Air Ministry announced very heavy German bombing. Though precise figures were not released, it was in fact the Luftwaffe's largest effort of the battle, with 1,786 sorties employing 500 bombers. The Germans lost 75 aircraft, compared with the loss of 34 British fighters. There was huge damage, particularly in the East End, with 300 civilians killed and 1,300 injured. Goering telephoned his wife, telling her triumphantly, "London is in flames".

As the battle in the skies wavered to and fro, the British Government issued an invasion warning. On 15 September we received this signal from the Commander-in-Chief, Western

Approaches, to all ships in his command:

> There is every indication that the enemy is about to attempt the invasion of our country, on the success of which all his hopes are based. It is certain that the attack is being prepared with great thoroughness and that it will be launched with skill and strength, regardless of losses.
>
> It is very necessary that every ship shall be prepared for battle, and every officer and man ready to answer any call. I am gratified to note the progress already made in the preparedness, which will be worthily maintained, to make good the defects and repairs to ships which happen to be in dockyard hands, and that everyone will do his utmost in the defence of his King and Country. Under the providence of God the attempt to invade our country will once more be brought to naught and the enemy will be given a smashing blow from which he will never recover.
>
> Knowing, as I do, the spirit of high courage and determination with which every officer and man is imbued, I am confident that the high tradition of our service will be maintained.

That same day the Air Ministry, as I remember vividly, reported news which lifted our spirits: the RAF had shot down 185 German aircraft. It was a gross overstatement. Liddell Hart, from British and German documents, gives the actual German losses as 60. Wild overestimates were regularly put out by both sides. But in this case the RAF lost only 26 fighters, with half of the pilots saved. The balance had begun to swing decisively in Britain's favour. Despite Goering's claims that he was on the point of destroying the RAF's fighter force, Hitler agreed with his admirals and generals. *Sealion* was postponed and in fact abandoned. Hitler's thoughts were now turning in the direction of Russia.

It was not the end of the blitz, which continued till May 1941. Night bombing of London continued for 57 nights continuously. Britain had suffered far more damage and had come nearer

15

to defeat than had been admitted. But the Luftwaffe had failed in its two main objects: the destruction of the RAF's fighter force and the breakdown of the British people's morale. Had there been media coverage comparable to that in the Vietnam war, who can tell what would have happened? But it was a different world.

To me and many of my friends, Britain's declaration of war had come as a huge relief after the era of appeasement, betrayal and shame. Churchill's accession as Prime Minister focused and fortified the spirit of defiance. His speeches, directed to Britain and the world, were timed and phrased to perfection. His tribute to the hard-pressed fighter-pilots at the height of the battle had a touch of genius: "Never in the field of human conflict was so much owed by so many to so few".

Churchill embodied and articulated a spirit which was already there. Liddell Hart has described the British people as instinctively stubborn and strategically ignorant.

> Churchill's inspiring speeches helped to correct the depression of Dunkirk and supplied the tonic the islanders wanted. They were exhilarated by his challenging note, and did not pause to ask whether it was strategically warranted ... Never was their collective characterisation as a bulldog so clearly demonstrated, in all its sublime stupidity.

The distinguished Australian historian, Sir Keith Hancock, was clear that in 1939 the overwhelming majority of the people of Britain supported a war designed to prevent Hitler stamping his image on the world. Hitler, baffled, turned, as Napoleon had done, to his long-term obsession: the conquest of Russia as a preliminary to a final settlement with Britain.

So, having done our bit to repel the invasion, we were ordered back to Northern Ireland for the equally crucial and far longer drama: the battle of the Atlantic. France had fallen, the Nazi-Soviet pact was in force, President Roosevelt had declared his policy to keep the United States out of the war. When France surrendered, German supporters in America held a celebratory party at New York's Waldorf-Astoria Hotel. Joseph Kennedy, the American Ambassador in London, was assuring Washington that Britain stood no chance of defeating Germany. It took the Japanese attack on Pearl Harbour to bring America into the war. Until then Britain, with the support of the Commonwealth countries, stood alone.

Earlier I had written a sonnet which *The Times* published on 18 July, 1940:

The Prophetic Hour

In this dread hour for thee and all mankind,
Britain, be Freedom's fortress or her grave.
There is no middle way. Conquer and save
The world, no less: fail, and the chains that bind
Our folk shall fetter body, soul and mind
Of all men everywhere. Fateful and brave
Such fight! But if we fail? Hell's flag shall wave
O'er Freedom's self to nether dark consigned.

One thing is needful: turn to God, whose laws
Are everlasting. Whom we own in part,
Obey: His yoke is perfect liberty.
To Him in humble trust commit our cause
And we shall see Hell's tyrant burst his heart
And the whole world start up, amazed, and free.

For some readers today the Miltonic style and archaic language may be a stumbling-block. But in the perspective of fifty-eight years of subsequent history, I see no reason to amend the theme.

CHAPTER 3

ROBERT'S LIFE AND DEATH

Our return from Dartmouth to Northern Ireland and the Atlantic convoys was matched by a sharp change in the season and weather.

As autumn moved into winter we began to encounter biting winds, sombre skies, occasional flurries of snow. Qualms attacked me as to how I would cope with trawler life in heavy weather. Hitherto all my seafaring had been in calm weather and sheltered waters. My mind went back to days of sea-sickness in the Australian Bight, and that in a passenger ship of 12,000 tons. Trawlers were notorious. The addition of a gun-platform and depth charges had increased their natural tendency to roll. The bane of sea-sickness has been acknowledged down the ages: the Duke of Medina-Sidonia was reluctant to accept command of the Spanish Armada as he was subject to it; and Nelson himself was not immune.

Tentatively I sounded out my mentor, Brian, on the subject. He grinned sardonically. "Most people feel pretty *quiet* on the first day or two at sea. Put it this way: if Hedy Lamarr appeared beside your bunk in her nightdress, you'd say, 'Not tonight, thank you'."

Individuals varied greatly. Some of our ex-fishermen could drink black tea that had been boiled for hours on the galley stove without turning a hair. One of them told me, "Strawberry jam's the stuff, Sir. Only thing that tastes the same coming up as going down".

In fact I was relieved to find that I could tolerate the rolling and pitching at least as well as most. Also that, although I had needed treatment before I could pass the eyesight test for the Navy, my night-vision was good, a critical matter for wartime night navigation.

My friendship with Brian grew. He was a man of high principles. In Belfast he had fallen for a charming girl whom he intended to marry. He invited her on board to meet us. She was pretty, sparkling and intelligent and seemed in every way suitable.

18

However, as an older married man, I felt it incumbent on me to have a serious word with him about the need for adequate time, consideration and perspective before taking such an important step. Brian listened with amiable attention but without comment. Soon afterwards I received an invitation to their wedding.

While we were busy with our convoy work from Derry into the Atlantic, November slid into December, and Honor's pregnancy drew nearer its completion date.

She stayed on at Burnfoot, with Tinny as helpful as ever, but she had much to carry, physically and mentally. Our families in Australia wrote, eager and anxious, amid news of war and bombings, awaiting the arrival of their first grandchild.

Neither Honor nor I knew anything about babies. Now she had to make all decisions and preparations without me. Amid the darkness and cold of oncoming winter, she lost other allies. Her great friend Sylvia left Britain for America and Australia. Virginia in Glasgow had advised on baby clothes and recommended a good Edinburgh obstetrician. But now Virginia also sailed for America with her children as bombings loomed, and the obstetrician was evacuated to a temporary hospital in Dumfries, south of Ardrossan, where Honor would need to go for the birth. "When the time came," she recalls, "I packed all my personal things and thought, Well, I would have to bring the baby back there. There didn't seem to be anywhere else to go." Her loyal friend Mary Hunter escorted her by train to Dumfries.

Meanwhile I had managed to get leave for the expected birth-date, 20 December. We stayed in a hotel for a week, while her pyjama cord would hardly meet in front; but there was no movement and I had to go back to the ship. Two days later, labour pains began.

I was able to telephone from Derry. Robert was born on 28 December, and jubilant telegrams sped to families and friends around the world. I went off to sea with the assurance that all was well with them both.

A Scottish schoolmaster and his wife, whom she had never met before, were her saviours. In her memoirs, Honor recalled them and the agony of those days when I was away on convoy duty in the Atlantic.

Without these friends, John and Milly Gall, I don't know what I would have done.

I was supposed to have a private room. Well, this turned out to be an enormous bare room, freezing cold, no carpets on the floor, no curtains; just the most bare necessities and one bed in the middle of it all. It seems extraordinary in the light of standards these days, but I was left with my pains by myself in that room for a very long time. Occasionally a nurse would come in and see if I was still alive, but it went on and on. I have never felt so utterly on my own. However, it came to an end and the baby was born and, again, I was overwhelmed by the most irrational bliss, bathed in it; I felt absolutely ecstatic and I didn't care a bit that I was left on the labour couch for I don't know how long after he arrived. They took him away of course. In those days the child was taken and cleaned up and only when presentable and wrapped up again was it presented to its mother.

At the same time in the same labour ward there was a girl having her baby. I tried to make conversation with her, but she would hardly talk and she was terrified during the labour process. I learned later that she was having an illegitimate baby and had no idea of what was to happen to her or to the baby after it was born. Also, beside me in the ward when I returned to it, there was a Canadian service wife in the next door room. I heard sounds of great grief and it turned out that her baby had been stillborn. This was in January in Scotland and I think the cold is the thing I remember more than anything else and these very starched sisters coming in and out. There was only one that I really felt at liberty to express any humanity at all to. They were all extremely professional. However, our little Robert had arrived, and that was the main thing, and my great friend, Milly Gall, came to call and keep in touch at all possible visiting hours.

As the days went by I wasn't very happy about the baby and there was no one I could talk to. The obstetrician appeared every so often — I don't think it was very often — and I asked the sisters if there was anything wrong with him. One of them said, "If you ask no questions, you will be told no lies". The baby soon got a cold and was most reluctant to feed and the combination of that and the freezing air very soon brought on cracked nipples, one of the most painful things when you are trying to help a baby to take his nourishment. By the twelfth day I began to feel that there was something desperately wrong and it was such an extraordinary situation for a woman like me who had been really so spoilt all her life. If anything was wrong with us at home, as when I had diphtheria, everything was laid on, a special trained nurse at home and consultations with all the other medicos, and here there was no reference point.

I think in their excitement at getting the best obstetrician, there had been no thought of a paediatrician and there was no such thing in the hospital. By the eighteenth day, January 14, it was right near the end. Just a day before that the obstetrician came in and spoke to me and told me that they had diagnosed what was wrong: it was an infection of the kidney, whether congenital or infected I was never to know. The result was that he went very, very yellow and then very, very blue, poor little mite. One night I heard him crying, I could recognise his cry, and I went along the corridor and there in a laboratory with a gas fire burning they had his little crib in front of the fire trying to keep some warmth around him. Fortunately, when the last moments came, I was allowed to get up and see him. They had a heating apparatus going and he was stripped naked and that was the only time I ever saw him naked, and this woman, this nice Scottish lass, who had some feeling, was in charge and I watched him struggle for his last breath. Finally, she said in a soft Scottish voice, "He's away".

At that point a very officious matron bustled in and said, "Now kiss baby goodbye, dear," and I had just had enough and I burst out at her, "Can't you leave me alone with him now?" So they all withdrew. I just knelt down and gave him back to God, there was nothing else I could do. I didn't even have the confidence to gather him up in my arms. In some strange way, he belonged to the hospital. I just went back to bed.

I remember one grey afternoon, a black raven flew across the window croaking in a most ominous manner, and then when I went out for a walk to get some exercise. Of course I could have been out of the hospital by then. I wandered on fairly directionless and ended up at the cemetery. So I turned back and realised that it was going to be that way. The doctor, although not really expert in the baby situation, when he finally came and spoke to me was very human and also very real because they had had their own particular tragedy, when a three-month-old child had died of cot death, a very terrible thing for any family, and he told me this, so that I knew he was trying to convey that he understood what I was going through.

But above all, throughout that time, Milly's faithful and heart-whole friendship meant absolutely everything. In fact I think it saved my reason. She would visit me every day and I would tell her what I was feeling and she would reply with her own deep sympathy and faith. She was over forty and had never had a child, but she understood in the inspired way people do when they are in touch with God. No, I will never forget how much she saved me at that time. And then her open-hearted way of inviting me to come back and stay in their home. At the same time she had had another friend staying with her, Isobel Gallatly, who was due to go to the hospital, and she went a day or two before I went back to the Galls' home. Soon after, while I was sitting there trying to recover, she was due to bring her second baby home, with no problems, thank God.

But when I heard the movement at the front door and I knew that this was Isobel coming back with her baby I had a huge resistance to going to say hello. I just did not want to know, and as I sat there by the fire — I could still see the little mantelpiece as I was staring at it — a voice said in my heart, "If you close your heart now you will take a bitter turn. It's up to you to decide". I found myself getting to my feet and joining Milly at the front door to welcome Isobel and her baby, and there seemed to come a healing out of that. I realised that in the past I'd never been very interested in small babies, very young babies. Of course Robert was different, passionately different. But now, after that small decision, I suddenly found I had a love for all babies, and that was a transformation in my nature and an enriching in my life from then on.

While Honor was going through this, I was out in the Atlantic, knowing nothing. It was a dreary but uneventful convoy. Then, on the last night of the homeward journey we had one of those unpredictable gifts which happen even in mid-ocean: a calm sea, with a crystal clear, breathtaking night of stars. In my duty-watch we had to see the last ships of the convoy safely into the Clyde, then turn and head back to base at Derry.

Only then could I get to telephone Milly and hear how things were.

My poem *Coming into the Clyde* seemed to write itself:

> Part of me for ever is the January morning
> Coming into the Clyde in the frosty moonlight
> And the land under snow and the snow under moonlight,
> Fall upon fall, a soundless ecstasy.
>
> I alone on the bridge, below me the helmsman
> Whistling softly to the listening voicepipe,
> And no sound else but the washing of the bow-wave
> As the buoys go by like marching pylons.
>
> I gaze from the glory of the bared universe
> To the guarded secret of the winter world
> Rapt, and the helmsman now is silent,

And I wait for the time to alter course.

To port lift the magic scenario mountains
White above the shoulders of Holy Island,
And nearer, clear as a square-lined coverlet,
All the fields and hedges on the slopes of Arran.

But further and smaller, away to starboard,
The plaited hills of Ayrshire gleam,
And I in thought am over them all
Away to my darling and my little son.

Beyond the moonlit hills that morning
My darling lay, and my little son;
But she in her cold bed lone and waking,
And he in the frozen ground asleep.

When we berthed in Derry and I got to a telephone, Milly
Gall's kind Scottish voice spoke. "She's all right; but I'm afraid
the baby has died. We're with her."

I rushed back to the ship to ask for leave. I had already had
a week and we might be ordered out to sea quite soon. There was
a pause. Lowe hesitated. Brian said, "I'll do watch and watch if
need be".

Sitting in the train to Larne, to catch the ferry for Stranraer,
I felt numb, far-away; but the wheels beat out, "She's all right,
she's all right". That was about all I could manage. By the time
I got to Dumfries I had focused. "Thank God, and keep up
morale." The baby whom I had never seen, and would never see,
had been buried in Dumfries cemetery. But his mother remembered him, "fair as the lily flower".

I found Honor staying with a kind friend and longing to see
me, as I her. But a chasm stood between us. Friends have said,
"The experience must have brought you closer," but immediately
the opposite was true. Honor told me, years afterwards, "You
came through the door cracking jokes". In totally unknown

24

territory all I could think of was keeping positive and cheerful. When I went back to the ship she was not resentful, but hurt and bewildered. I wrote a poem.

Surmise

My little son, whose face I never saw,
Who could not wait to bless your father's eyes
With wonder, but in such mysterious wise
Slipped from our world bound hard by frost and war
But warm for you with love, in silent awe
We ponder, in a shrouded deep surmise,
Your swifter summons to the world that lies
In our own path, beyond the selfsame door.

Was there a need, some work there, sudden and great,
Your work? Of do you there prepare our home?
Lest we be timid, touched with fear and sin,
Will you beside that mighty portal wait?
Who, when your father and your mother come,
Will take us by the hand and lead us in.

I was struggling to express the love, loss and mystery we both felt with the hope and promises we both believed. Years later I searched further, trying to accept, rather than resolve, a profound mystery.

Genesis

You spoke, after long years, about the morning
That followed the night your first-born son was born:
The dead of winter, the wartime emergency hospital
Bare, spare, necessitous, institutional,
Quick voices, hurrying feet, then seas of silence,
Snow building building against the window pane,
You under a blanket, bathed in ecstasy.

This only: he who was to come had come —
No other thing, on earth or out of time.
Beyond the pane, the winter world at war
Endless and dark, where you must lay your child;
Within, no one of all your dearest few,
Belonging cheek or voice, to share your light,
Seas, continents away — all this, yet all
Caught upward in your solar storm of bliss
For joy a man was born into the world.

You spoke, re-living that release of light
That sank so soon to darkness, pain and death.
I groped, questioned, astray, not comprehending,
Asking in vain, with words of another world.
You turned away, for you could tell no more.

O let the taloned mind let go its quarry
And let the proud mind fall with Lucifer
Because it is another kind of dimension
And the leap forward is kneeling in one place
And the answer is given silently to no question
And they who ask, in anger or pain of spirit,
Why ever a dead planet was torn to life
Come if they will to mother and child — for she
Because she is the ark of the covenant
Can neither tell nor know a need to tell.

Healing came in time. Robert, in his short life, had taken us into
waters wider and deeper than the Atlantic.

CHAPTER 4

COME DEATH SUDDENLY

Come death suddenly from the sea or cloud
With the blast of thunder and the blinding shroud,
With the wild sea spinning as the heavens fall ...

I wrote these lines after my first experience of enemy action, in the summer of 1941. As so often with naval encounters, it was a brief, intense episode in the midst of long stretches of peaceful, monotonous passage.

Not always monotonous. "This is the kind of thing people pay thousands of pounds to do in peace-time," I wrote to Honor. We were cruising up through the romantically beautiful Western Isles of Scotland, some of them with names as knotted and nobbly as a crummock, such as Eigg, Rum and Muck, amid views of magic and poetry. The title of one Admiralty chart we used was "From Ardnamurchan to the Summer Isles": a perfect pentameter line.

My situation had changed. Having qualified for my "watch-keeping certificate", I had been promoted to Lieutenant, had said goodbye to *Northern Dawn* friends, and had been appointed First Lieutenant ("Number One": Executive Officer) of *Gavotte*, an Admiralty-built trawler, rather like a miniature corvette, one of the "Dance Class", with sisters named *Sarabande, Fox Trot* and the like. Based in Belfast, our job was to escort convoys from Oban, the peace-time yachting resort, now a major convoy rendezvous, up the west coast, across the top of Scotland, through the Pentland Firth and down the east coast to Edinburgh.

With summer days and sheltered waters, the first part of our journey was often a picnic. When off watch I could read in comfort in my small cabin, or practise my recorder (sometimes to cries from shipmates of "Where's that snake charmer?"). My new CO, Booker, from the south of England, was affable, sociable and relaxed, so much so that a new and nervous Sub, who had the morning watch (4 am to 8 am) was put to the test. As we cruised through a smooth but very narrow channel, he became alarmed at the course he had been given, and called down anxiously to a sleeping Captain, "Sir, I'm afraid if we keep this course we'll be on the rocks".

A drowsy voice replied up the voice-pipe, "What's that, Sub?"

"If we keep on this course, Sir, we'll be on the rocks."

A long pause; then, "Well, steer some other course".

People differ. We avoided catastrophe.

At Oban, Booker, as usual, went ashore to meet the Commodore (Senior Officer) of the Convoy and other officers of his ship, SS *Forthbank*, as well as to co-ordinate convoy arrangements. They had a convivial hotel lunch; Booker told me what an exceptionally nice bunch they were and mentioned a keen young apprentice who had particularly impressed him. Next day, as we steamed north past the isle of Skye, the shadows of clouds were climbing in procession up the wonderful heather-clad mountain slopes.

Rounding Cape Wrath, we made our way across the north of Scotland, and altered course to cross the Moray Firth, heading southward. *Gavotte*'s station was on the seaward side at the head of the convoy, parallel with the Commodore in *Forthbank*. From experience of the convoys we had been warned what we must be ready for. Across the North Sea, at Stavanger in Norway, the Germans had a seaplane base which launched attacks on the convoys. There was one crucial day, and one crucial period, just before nightfall, when the line of ships could be sharply silhouetted against the setting sun, and low-flying planes from eastward could approach unseen. We had no radar so eyesight was everything. "You're lucky if you get ten seconds' warning," we had been told. In mid-afternoon an escorting sloop signalled that she had sighted a German plane far off on the horizon. No doubt we had been reported.

Two RAF fighters had been flying cheerfully round the convoy; but just before dusk, as we closed up to Action Stations, they had to leave and return to base. It was eerie, electric, almost like going on tiptoe; each minute brought us nearer to darkness and safety. My station was on the port wing of the bridge, with the seaman who manned one of our Lewis guns, as we peered into the thickening gloom. Then it happened: a line of red tracer bullets coming straight at us, as our return fire met theirs like swords crossing. I had two reflexes: a kind of outrage that for the first time in my life someone was firing deliberately at me; and discovery of my gift for the non-heroic. I found myself crouching automatically behind a strip of canvas which gave no protection whatsoever. A few fierce, hectic seconds, then the plane, now visible and low, veered away into the darkness ahead.

We had not been hit, but soon we saw his main target. From *Forthbank*, half a mile away, two Lewis guns on the bridge blazed furiously at the German as, firing his own guns, he came in from ahead at mast height. His bombs struck the foredeck, blowing the whole bridge structure over the side, and starting a fierce fire. The plane itself, as we found afterwards, had then dived into the sea and sunk. Whether this was a result of counter-fire or pilot's error will never be known.

Anxiously we waited, but there were no further attacks. The rest of the convoy steamed on past us towards Edinburgh, and we were left with *Forthbank*. We could see the fire and men on her well-deck. Booker could not leave the bridge. It was my job, as Number One, to investigate. We came close, lowered a boat, and pulled across. A ladder was lowered and I climbed up the steep side to the deck. A bundle of rags and blood lay in the scuppers, the headless body, they told me, of the young apprentice. The Commodore and all the bridge personnel had been killed by the bomb. The survivors were steady and cool. "We've got no engines and no pumps for the fire. Can you help us?"

I reported back to Booker. Keen to help, he was also responsible for the safety of his own ship and ship's company. But we couldn't hold back. We brought *Gavotte* alongside the still burning *Forthbank*, passed our canvas hoses up to the men on deck, and began pumping. Only the calm weather made it possible; but it worked. After a couple of hours they had the fire under control. *Forthbank* was seaworthy and could be towed to harbour when daylight came and tugs could reach her. Shocked, shaken and subdued, we set course for Edinburgh. "We had lunch together yesterday," mumbled Booker.

For the present at least, *Forthbank* was not one of the 4,786 merchant ships that would be lost in the six years of war. But the Commodore and his staff were among the 32,000 men of the Merchant Navy who would die in that war. A Memorial on Tower Hill, London, records their names, and that they

> Gave their lives for their country
> And have no grave but the sea.

During subsequent trips we had a number of alarms, but were in no further attacks. Conditions and tides meant that we had to follow the same general timetable: each time that we "darkened ship" and closed up to Action Stations off the same stretch of Scotland's east coast, nerves would become tense and conversations minimal, until the saving darkness fell.

"Chuck another lump of coal on, Chief," Booker called down the voicepipe to the engine-room. "We want to get in for a quiet night." The Chief responded, and we put on a few more revs. Homeward bound, we had safely delivered our ships to the anchorage at Oban, and were looking forward to a relaxed night in our cosy little berth in the Pollock Dock, Belfast. As we secured alongside, I thought of a leisurely meal, our snug wardroom, and the luxury of pyjamas.

It was not to be. In their methodical campaign of bombing British ports, the Luftwaffe had made Belfast, hitherto spared, their objective for the night. The surprise, as far as we were concerned, was complete. As the sirens wailed and searchlights wavered over the sky, we manned our two Lewis guns, then realised it was a pointless exercise, and sent the men below for shelter. The planes came over one after the other, at a high level, out of range of any weapons we had. There had been no warning or time to move out into the Lough; now it would be foolish and dangerous. Our role was simply to be a target, as inconspicuous as we could manage, without the psychological relief of action. It was a test few of us had yet experienced.

The attack began at 11 pm, and went on till 5 am. The main target seemed to be the centre of the city. Soon it was a blazing inferno, as planes droned overhead, bombs whistled down, stoking the fires, and buildings could be seen burning and collapsing half way round our horizon, as smoke billowed up into the sky. Never voiced, but in all our minds was the thought, "Will the next one be for us?" Some of the crew began to crack; one was the young steward.

Then it was that the Cox'n, Pitt, older than most of them, showed his real quality. Formerly Bosun of a peace-time yacht, he was a superb seaman, invaluable in his experience, but also a leader with a fatherly touch. Amid the noise, shocks and flashes he poked his head into the wardroom: "I've just been down talking to the lads in the mess. Told 'em not to worry," to which he added, "Come round with me, sir — cheers 'em up". As he and I went round the ship together, his flow of breezy, matter-of-fact patter never stopped. There was a whistle and an explosion that shook the ship.

"Whew, that was a close one, eh?"

"Yessir — that's a whistling bomb — simple thing, typical Jerry trick — meant to frighten you. The tail's just a bit o' cardboard with a hole in it ...

"Have a word with Cook and the others, sir, cheers 'em up ... Did I ever tell you ..."

His "cool" heartened all of us through that sleepless night. Pitt was Britain's best.

Just as day was dawning, Booker and I stepped out on deck. "That seems to be it," I said. At that moment we heard the whistling shriek of an approaching bomb and found ourselves instantly stretched out flat on the deck. The bomb fell near, but seemed not to explode.

Presently we heard that a Base shore-party had found a hole in the nearby quay, and looking down had seen the shining black posterior of a bomb, evidently a dud, buried in the mud. They covered the hole, to prevent accidents. Then second thoughts occurred: dud, or time-bomb? We were told as a precaution to shift ship to the other side of the dock, 100 yards or so. As we secured in our new berth, the bomb exploded, throwing up tons of mud and timber, but doing no other damage.

This was the first of three raids on Belfast, but we were not in port for the others. We heard that as the German planes flew north to attack, fire-brigades from the officially neutral south of Ireland sped up to the assistance of their northern countrymen.

CHAPTER 5

IRISH INTERLUDE

May 1941 saw the end of Hitler's major blitz on Britain, which had caused crippling damage to Clydeside, Coventry, Portsmouth, Bristol, Plymouth, Liverpool and Merseyside and above all London where, on 10 May, five docks and all but one of the major railway stations had been put out of action, and the House of Commons destroyed by fire.

More than 94,000 civilians had been killed or seriously injured. The few in Whitehall who knew all these facts at the time also knew the need to maintain national morale, as well as keeping the enemy in the dark. For news we depended, like the rest of the country, on the BBC, which reported heavy raids but of course published no precise figures or details of damage. The bombing eased only because of the transfer of the Luftwaffe to the east, for the conquest of Russia, which Hitler planned to accomplish before the winter. He could then return to deal with Britain.

Those months in Belfast were a gift in many ways. I could keep in regular touch with Honor, by post and even telephone. She made progress in recovery from her grief over Robert's death. My brother Peter who, after taking his Oxford degree in Maths, had joined the Navy as an Ordinary Seaman, got leave and helped her final packing up from Burnfoot. She had been invited to stay at Tirley Garth, a beautiful country house in Cheshire which its owner, Irene Prestwich, had given as a country centre for the Oxford Group.

War had brought transformation to Tirley Garth. With a staff of indomitable land-girls who rose before dawn, it became a productive farm and market garden. While shipping losses were critical, Britain managed to grow two-thirds of its own food needs. Tirley Garth was untouched during the heavy bombing of Merseyside twelve miles away, though returning bombers sometimes unloaded at random in the neighbourhood. Honor shared a bedroom with several girls, worked in the kitchen, and sang in a chorus.

Belfast was a busy naval base, and had one of Britain's largest ship-building yards, Harland and Wolff. Being alongside the quay was not always restful. There was constant coming and going, with the arrival of stores, signals from the Base, chipping, painting and repairs not possible at sea. Social visitors from nearby ships had easy access. Shore-based officers who did not receive our supplies of duty-free liquor and cigarettes were particularly ready to relax in our wardroom and extend their glasses to receive "the other half" of whiskey, pink gin or gin-and-lime. *Gavotte* was a coal-burner, and to "coal ship" a crane would empty a railway-truck of coal on to our steel deck with a sound like thunder. The coal had to be shovelled away to bunkers, while coal-dust filled the air and blackened everything until hosed down.

One morning, while busy with such concerns, I received what seemed like a message from another planet. My mail included a gold-embossed letter from the Poet Laureate, John Masefield, saying that he was pleased to inform me that I had been awarded the King's Medal for Poetry. I was suitably pleased and totally surprised, as I had had no communication with Masefield, and did not know that he was aware of my existence. I had never heard of the King's Medal for Poetry. Ashamed of my ignorance, I resorted to a plan. I consulted the Chief Librarian at Belfast's Public Library. He could not enlighten me immediately, but kindly offered to make enquiries.

We went off on another convoy, and after we returned and docked I prepared to visit the Library. Before I could do so, I found another letter from the Poet Laureate waiting for me. It read, "The Public Librarian at Belfast has written to say that a young naval officer has been enquiring about the King's Medal for Poetry: could this possibly be you?" It was one of those pivotal moments in my life's pilgrimage, sending me back to Grade 1 schooldays and the popular copy-book inscription, "Honesty is the Best Policy".

Masefield was entirely gracious. He told me that the King's Medal for Poetry was an award given every three years for the work of a poet under thirty. Previous awards had been to Laurence

34

Whistler and W.H. Auden. At that point my only published work had been *Milton Blind*, the Newdigate Prize poem, which had been published by Blackwells of Oxford.

There was another link, as I now recalled. Masefield had spoken both to Trinity College and to Janet Clark Hall (where Honor had been a student) when he visited Melbourne for its Centenary celebrations in 1934; but we had not met personally.

We now became friends, and corresponded. I sent him a draft of my long ballad *The Jervis Bay*. He praised it, and made some suggestions, which I made bold to reject, but asked permission to dedicate the poem to him.

My Australian loyalties led to the one unresolved difference I had with Booker. He knew almost nothing about Australia, but he did know one thing, body-line: source of so much passionate and heated controversy between our two countries. I had not been a cricketer and was not versed in the finer points of the dispute, but I did remember my cricket-playing English headmaster, James Darling, muttering "Jardine's a stupid fool". I felt called upon to express what many Australians felt, particularly when our national hero, Bradman, was involved. Booker would have none of it. "You didn't like being beaten. Larwood was too good for you. That's all there was to it." From there he would not budge. Respecting the Naval tradition not to discuss religion round the wardroom table, we dropped the subject. We had a greater war on our hands. I hope Booker lived long enough to observe that Harold Larwood, after the war, came to Australia, was warmly welcomed, and settled here.

In Belfast I found special refreshment when it was possible, getting away from ship-board life and the dusty dockyard and taking a tram out to Wolfhill on a green slope on the northern fringe of the city, the home of Gordon and Hilda Hannon and their family. He was an Archdeacon of the Church of Ireland and their home was a meeting place for Oxford Group friends. Their welcome was unreserved. Often the open door brought a whiff of fresh baking, as Hilda was busy with a batch of her famed soda-bread, and the children ran in and out. Immediately they gave an invitation for Honor to visit when and if that was possible. Under their hospitable roof, I met Denis Hanna, a gifted architect, and his wife Nora, who later had us to stay in their home in Holywood across the Lough.

Gordon and Hilda were wholeheartedly committed to the Oxford Group's programme of changed lives as a basis for changing society. But they approached this as an interesting adventure rather than as a burdensome obligation. They readily accepted my invitation to visit the ship for drinks and meet my brother officers. It was a cordial occasion, Hilda chatting with great animation and Booker telling me afterwards how much he liked them. On the way home they were chuckling. Hilda told me, "Gordon doesn't drink, though he likes it. He asked for just lime juice, but the steward brought him gin and lime". I asked Gordon what he had done. He twinkled. "I drank it. I remembered the Scripture, 'Seek first the Kingdom of Heaven, and all these things shall be added unto you'."

Humour and reality often broke through in gatherings at Wolfhill. An elderly lady who had a large house near the border told of a bridge-building effort she had made. Her village football-team had been sent to play another village a few miles away in the Catholic South, as a move to promote friendship and solidarity. The returning team leapt from the train with triumphant cries: "We've won, we've won! There'll be sore hearts in the Vatican tonight!"

At Wolfhill I met Irish people from both North and South, equally dedicated to healing the centuries-old divisions of their troubled country.

For me, the stay in Ireland was relaxing and timely. At Tirley Garth and elsewhere in England I had sometimes felt a conscientious, dutiful intensity, even when I knew that the people concerned were leading unselfish and dedicated lives. Here the reduced pressure helped me to focus a conflict in my own spirit. I had never committed myself unreservedly to being part of the Oxford Group. Yet I had to admit that it represented the most wholehearted and convincing collection of people I had met in the struggle for the things which meant most to me. We were in the midst of a war to save a world worth living in. What right had I to withhold, withdraw, safeguard my precious ego? Telling no one, I knelt beside my bunk in *Gavotte*, decided to throw in my lot with the Oxford Group and its work, and asked God to help me. I wrote to Honor and told her. It was all quite matter-of-fact.

She came over to stay at Wolfhill and we had a memorable week's leave in the South, in the lovely Wicklow Mountains, visiting Glendalough and St Kevin's bed. The frontier was open: all I had to do was wear sports clothes instead of uniform. We heard there was a brisk trade from the food-rich South to the rationed North, including turkeys wrapped in babies' shawls. In Dublin we visited the museum which housed the memorials of "The Troubles", the bitter fighting that led to the emergence of the Irish Free State in 1922. We had the place to ourselves. As we wandered about, gazing at cases of weapons, flags and photographs, the curator, seeing our interest, came up and with flashing eyes recalled his part in those heroic days, including his own exploit of capturing a British armoured car. We were fascinated by his zest; but then said that our vision was of the day which saw the end not only of the present war, but of all wars.

"That's it!" he responded, "That's it — the brotherhood o' man!" How did he think we might get there? "Oh, there must be a bath o' blood. Through a bath o' blood, to the brotherhood o' man!" As we left, he beamed on us with genuine warmth, overflowing with the milk of human kindness.

Ireland had a part in another important step in our lives. After the loss of Robert and the months that followed, we had both felt we should try to have another child, and had told some friends. But nothing had ensued. Honor planned to return to Tirley Garth from Belfast, but before she left, Hilda Hannon arranged for us to stay a few days with relatives of hers on the rugged north coast I knew so well from seaward. It was windy and cloudy; but we were the only guests and could make our own timetable. We went for vigorous walks and came back to roaring fires and dinner, before it was time for bed.

Honor's health was fully restored, but on the smooth ferry-crossing from Larne to Stranraer she felt unaccountably queasy. There was no mystery. Robert's younger brother or sister had decided it was time to make a start.

CHAPTER 6

JERVIS BAY

Soon after we returned to Ireland in *Northern Dawn* from our Channel patrols during the Battle of Britain, the BBC reported a dramatic action in waters we knew.

On 5 November 1940 a convoy from Halifax to Britain, HX 84, was attacked in mid-Atlantic by the German pocket battleship *Admiral Scheer*. The sole escort, the armed merchant cruiser *Jervis Bay,* engaged the *Scheer* and was sunk, with the Captain and three-quarters of her company, but enabled 32 of the 37 ships in the convoy, which could well have been annihilated, to escape.

Churchill later wrote:

> The only thing that ever really frightened me during the war was the U-boat peril ... I was even more anxious about this battle than I had been about the glorious air fight called the Battle of Britain.

His stirring speeches gave no hint of this fear at the time. But it was clear to everyone that the Atlantic convoys were the vital lifeline on which Britain's survival depended.

Honor wrote to me from Scotland. "Why don't you write a ballad: 'Captain Fogarty Fegen sailed in the *Jervis Bay*'?"

Captain E.S. Fogarty Fegen, RN, the *Jervis Bay*'s Captain, was awarded a posthumous VC. Apart from his evocative Irish name, Honor's thought sparked an immediate fire in my imagination. I did not use her suggested first line, but kindling ideas came flying in from all points. Before the war, the ship and her sisters of the Aberdeen and Commonwealth Line — the "Bay Boats" — were well known to Australians as they plied their mixed passenger and cargo trade between Australian and British ports. My schoolfriend, David Hay, had travelled to England in the *Jervis Bay*. Jervis Bay, on the New South Wales coast, named after the famous Admiral Jervis, Nelson's senior, was the site of the Australian Navy's officer training college. Fegen had spent

39

three years as Commander there and had friends and relatives in Australia. Staff at the College felt proud of his gallant action, recognised in his VC.

The action itself struck a chord in me which had begun to vibrate when I was nine, when my father read to me, from *Lyra Heroica — a Book of Verse for Boys*, such epics of heroic sacrifice as "Horatius" and the ballad of the little *Revenge* confronting the fifty-three Spanish galleons. Moreover, the *Jervis Bay*'s twenty-two heroic minutes had not been a romantic, ineffectual gesture, but a substantial contribution to the survival of Britain.

I could live into those minutes because I had so often seen those columns of helpless merchant ships lumbering at 8 knots across the vast, inscrutable ocean. The comparison with a mob of defenceless sheep was irresistible. Like ships in which I was serving, *Jervis Bay* was an expedient, converted from routine peace-time functions to an unfamiliar war-time role. Her company, with a sprinkling of professionals, was a varied assortment, many still learning the ways of war and the sea, typifying a country caught less than half-prepared for war. Her main armament consisted of seven six-inch guns of World War I vintage. She had no armour, and a speed of less than 15 knots. The German pocket battleships, with a speed of 27 knots and armoured sides, had six eleven-inch guns; they had been designed to outgun British cruisers and outrun British battleships.

I began to collect everything I could learn about the ship and the action. By a bit of luck, I was able to visit Harland and Wolff's yard and see a similar conversion-job in progress. I was horrified. In our small ships, and especially with a Coxswain like Pitt, we reckoned, without any slave-driving, to keep every man usefully busy in working hours. But in the shipyard, I observed gangs of dockyard "mateys", after shuffling up the gangway, making their way to the messdecks and whiling away happy hours at cards or brewing tea, apparently at infinite leisure.

It was not my business to interfere with dockyard management. But in the first draft of my ballad, picturing *Jervis Bay*'s conversion (which had been at Tyneside, not Belfast), I recorded what I had seen. This passage caused consternation with the Admiralty censors, who feared an adverse effect on public morale. In the end we came to a compromise, using the operative word "yet", with the lines:

A dockyard matey working was a sight you rarely saw;
Yet when they left the *Jervis Bay* she was a ship of war.

I had a moving account from a friend, Commander Frederick B. Watt of the Royal Canadian Navy, himself a poet and author, who had been at the convoy conference in Halifax before HX 84 sailed. Fegen had spoken to the merchant captains, saying, "If we meet another armed merchant cruiser, I believe we'll give a good account of ourselves. If we should meet a German warship, this is what I shall do ...".

Watt told me, "From the moment we got the first signal, we seemed to be watching the acting out of something we had seen before".

Fegen had told his crew: "If we meet the enemy I shall take you in as close as I possibly can". A young sailor had said, "I think we'd follow old Fogarty anywhere". Fegen could have had no doubt about what his decision involved. A year earlier the armed merchant cruiser *Rawalpindi* had been sunk by two German cruisers: there were only 38 survivors.

I wrote to the Admiralty telling of my project and requesting permission to study the official records. Weeks ran into months, and I got no reply. Then I heard that I was being appointed to a new ship in Iceland. On a brief leave in London I told my situation and shared my frustration with Jerry Anderson, a Lieutenant Commander RN who used to drop in regularly at the Oxford Group headquarters at Hays Mews. He thought a while, then said, "Ah". He rang his friend, Tony Kimmins, the playwright, also RN and working in the appropriate area in Whitehall. No difficulty. "The records you want are down those stairs, on the left. When you've finished, let yourself out to the street and bang the door." I read and made notes on the reports of the *Jervis Bay* survivors. Specially vivid and detailed was the long, handwritten account by the First Lieutenant. His was the recollection that as the *Jervis Bay* finally went down, the hot barrel of the last gun hissed into the waves of the Atlantic.

From various sources the picture of Fegen continued to build up: a 47-year old bachelor, devout Roman Catholic from an Irish family, inheritor of the Navy's traditions through his grandfather, a Captain, and father, a Vice-Admiral. In *Jervis Bay* he continued the determination of his predecessor to make it a happy ship's company. He tried to get to know each man, dropped the formality of being piped aboard (traditional for COs), attended ship's concerts, played a drum in the band, and mixed well with the Merchant Navy officers.

Dark, strongly built and handsome, he was remembered as an enthusiast for physical fitness when Commander at Jervis Bay Naval College. He made friends in Australia but followed the tradition of the "Silent Service" where his personal life was concerned. Years later I heard from a colleague, Captain Eric Nave, about an episode on the China station when Fegen was Commander of the cruiser *Suffolk* and Eric was Admiral's secretary. Hearing that *Suffolk* (their junior) possessed a particularly useful Chinese laundry, which the Admiral coveted, Eric asked Fegen over to lunch. Eric began tentative enquiries, but Fegen cut him short: "Eric, you surely didn't ask me to lunch to get hold of our laundry! I'll never believe that — never!" The laundry stayed in *Suffolk*.

I finished my ballad while on passage by transport to Iceland, to join my new ship *Wastwater*. Appropriately, the first reading took place in the home of our friends Denis and Nora Hanna, in Belfast, where the poem had its first germination. As required for all Service personnel, I submitted my text to the Admiralty censor, and duly received his approval for its publication. In 1942 it was the title-piece for my first book, *The Jervis Bay and other Poems*, published by Putnams in New York and London. Four thousand copies were sold, including sales in Australia, New Zealand and Canada.

Some time after publication I received a long-delayed reply to my letter requesting permission to see the Admiralty records. It informed me that, as my poem was intended for publication, my request could not be approved.

Since then, the poem has been continuously in print, in my own collections and in a number of anthologies. In poetry readings which I have given over the years I have usually included a passage from it; and often have been aware of unmistakable response. Not always has this response sprung from literary considerations alone. In 1996, when my pianist daughter Penelope and I gave a music-and-poetry recital in the San Anton Palace, Malta, the President flung his arms round me and exclaimed, "We know all about the *Jervis Bay!* The *Jervis Bay* used to come to Malta!"

In writing, as in everything else, time and circumstances alter values. When, after the war, I joyfully packed away my uniform in favour of the de-mob suit and baggy sports clothes, a subtle change began. By the time we were back in Melbourne and I found myself absorbed in learning my new role as university lecturer, exposed to the finer points of literary criticism and aware of all that I did not know, I was more affected than I realised by the change of scene. I felt almost apologetic. Among my new colleagues, only one had been in the services, as an Army Education Officer. In our morning coffee-breaks I talked, perhaps too much, about my naval experience. I don't remember anyone referring to *The Jervis Bay*. Absorbed in exploring with my classes G.M. Hopkins' innovations in verse rhythm, and the brilliant "conceits" of Donne and the metaphysicals, I unconsciously downgraded *The Jervis Bay* to the status of just a ballad. I had yet to learn the tyranny of literary fashion and of subservience to the assumed authority of contemporary gurus.

In 1941 I sent my first draft to Masefield, asking permission to dedicate the poem to him. While praising the drama of the story, he suggested that I should streamline the narrative to make it faster-moving, by dropping the passage invoking heroic actions of the past, and should also omit the sheep and sheep-dog metaphor. I felt that this would impoverish the poem, which suggests that gallant and sacrificial acts are somehow outside time as we understand it. Similarly, the sheep and sheep-dog image is directly linked with the tenth chapter of St John's gospel, where Jesus contrasts the hireling who runs away when he sees the wolf coming with the good shepherd who lays down his life for the sheep.

A number of listeners, including some children, have mentioned the sheep and sheep-dog story as their favourite passage. For some anthologists, including Kenneth Baker in his recent *Faber Book of War Poetry*, the immediacy of the action has been the main interest. For his naval section, his excerpts, along with passages from *The Jervis Bay*, are from John Donne, Andrew Marvell, and John Dryden, each writing of events close to his own time.

On the other hand, Rosalind Russell, editor of *Literary Links* (between Australia and Britain) chose the reflective passage focused on Fegen's moment of choice, "ranked with other heroic and decisive moments of history".

For the Penguin edition of *The Voice of War*, an anthology of poems by men and women who served in World War II, edited by Victor Selwyn, I made an abridgement of the whole poem, particularly in order to include all the elements of the original.

The Jervis Bay has certainly created more unusual and unexpected links over the last 55 years than anything else I have written.

From *The Jervis Bay* — Fegen engages the enemy

"Hard-a-port" and "Hard-a-port, sir." The white spray flying,
She heeled and turned and steadied her course for where the foe was
    lying
"Salvoes, fire" Her guns speak, but they are old and worn,
The shots fall in the water, short. The raider as in scorn
Keeps his fire on the convoy still, now veiled in smoke, now clear,
But the Jervis Bay is closing fast and her shots are creeping near.
And now he swings on her his turrets, as a thief surprised might turn.
His anger thunders near, ahead. She trembles from stem to stern.
A flash, and she staggers, as through her egg-shell plates
Tear the eleven-inch projectiles, malevolent as the Fates,
And smoke pouring and wreckage flying as the shells fall like rain,
But she fights, and the convoy are scattering fast, and every minute
    is gain.
"Am closing the enemy," Fegen signals. She heaves, and is hit again.

Now the wolf is among the flock,
The sheep are leaping to ledge and rock
Like scattered clouds. To left and right
The wolf is at work and his teeth are white,
His teeth are white and quick is he.
Soon the flock will cease to be
That grazed along so peaceably.

But suddenly the sheepdog comes
With growling as a roll of drums,
Stiff and heavy, eyes a-blear,
But he knows the wolf is near
And within the aged brain
One thought only may remain,
Headlong as he hurls himself
At the grey throat of the wolf
Where his old teeth sink and stay.

But he, with fury and dismay,
Drops his kill and turns to tear
The creature that affronts him there.
This way and that he rends and claws
But cannot break those ancient jaws
That never while they live relax,
While flanks are torn and sinew cracks
And haunch a mangled tatter lies
And the blood runs in his eyes
And hanging so, he dies.
And it is cold and it is night
Before the finish of the fight
When the panting wolf shakes free
From the bloody corpse, and he
Lies like a sack, defaced and dead,
And the sheep into the hills are fled
And the wolf slinks to his bed.

Now the Jervis Bay is ablaze. The fo'c's'le is blown away.
Splinters rive her decks to ribbons and bury her under spray,
And her burning hull as she plunged on was a bright torch that day.
She shudders. With the clearing smoke her main bridge is gone,
And Fegen's arm is a shredded stump, and he fights on.
He staggers aft to the docking bridge. Another blinding blast.
The Ensign down. "Another Ensign! Nail it to the mast."
A seaman climbs and nails it there, where the House Flag used to fly,
And there it speaks defiance to the shaker of the sky.
He strives to climb to the after bridge, but it is unavailing,
One arm and half the shoulder gone, and strength fast failing.
But there is still the after gun that he can bring to bear.
"Independent fire!" he cries, as heaves into the air
The after bridge. He lives, and staggers forrard again, before
The rolling smoke envelops him, and he is seen no more.

Now her engines had ceased to turn, but still the shells came pouring
Till with a roar her boilers burst, and the white steam went soaring
Away to the sky. Her back was broken, and she was settling fast,

46

And the fire blazed, and the smoke-pall brooded like a banyan vast,
But still the torn Ensign flew from the black stump mast,
And the after gun was firing still and asking no quarter
When the hot barrel hissed into the wild grey water.

So ended the fight of the Scheer and the Jervis Bay
That for twenty vital minutes drew the raider's fire that day,
When of the convoy's thirty-seven, thirty-two went safe away
And home at last to England came, without the Jervis Bay.

But now thick night was over the sea, and a wind from the west blew
    keen,
And the hopeless waters tossed their heads where the Jervis Bay had
    been,
And the raider was lost in the rain and the night, and low clouds hid
    the seas,
But high above sea and storm and cloud appeared the galaxies,
The Bear, Orion, myriad stars that timeless vigil keep,
A glimmering host the stars came out across the heaving deep,
And they shone bright over the good shepherd of sheep.

CHAPTER 7

SHIP AND SHIPMATES

At anchor in Reykjavik Roads.

"We'll have a few days clear, anyway," reported the Captain on his return from Operations. "There's nothing immediate for us. We can grant the usual shore leave. I've sent for Chief. How's the paper war?"

I pushed across a pile of signals which had arrived in his absence; their subject-matter ranged from the boundaries of minefields to the programme of last week's ENSA concert.

"North-westerly gale expected. Nothing much else." The Captain sank into a chair, tossed his cap on the wardroom table and glanced through the sheaf of paper. "Well, we'd better veer out some more cable. Glad we're not at sea tonight, anyway."

A shadow darkened the doorway. "Ah, Chief," said the Captain, looking up, "we're at four hours' notice for steam, so you can get on with any small jobs you want to do in the engine room. You mentioned something."

"Aye. There's them piston rings of dynamo engine; and Ah've a couple o' glands need re-packin'."

"Right. And, er, Chief, when you get time, you might look at my shower; the hot water doesn't seem to work, and the cold water comes out all rusty."

A gleam of interest lightened the Chief's countenance. "Aye, I'll have a look at 'er in mornin': strip 'er right down like."

A shadow of apprehension passed over the Captain's face, but he nodded assent. Those were early days, and we had not yet experienced the full force of the Chief's enthusiasm for stripping down and blanking off: treatment which he prescribed for any mechanical ailment with the gusto of an eighteenth century physician ordering purges or blood-letting. He melted away, while the Captain thought hopefully of the benefits of an efficient hot shower. He would have done better to meditate with Dr Johnson upon the Vanity of Human Wishes.

The days at anchor ran into weeks. Considering the weather

we were not sorry, and it was a useful opportunity to get the ship cleaned up after the turmoil of refit. Apart from the essential expeditions for provisions, naval stores, or on ship's business, we went ashore little. The weather was too bad to use our own boats, so our only touch with the shore was the small "trot-boat" which chugged its way laboriously round the anchorage. After one or two trips standing on its wet, windy deck, competing with numerous other voices all pleading with the Icelandic skipper for priority in visiting their various ships, my enthusiasm for shore-going waned. Jumping at last onto *Wastwater*'s welcome deck, our hearts would warm to the domestic emotion of "Home, Home, Never More to Roam". Thereafter it took some special inducement, such as a new consignment of paint, or a wangle of some green baize for the wardroom table.

Those who have served in a number of ships often retain a special feeling about a particular one. But when I joined HMS *Wastwater* in Iceland in October 1941 I had no intuition that she was going to be "my" ship in a way that no other ever quite was.

Once again I was posted as First Lieutenant. *Wastwater* was similar in size to my previous trawlers but with significant differences. Built in Britain in 1939 for the Norwegian whaling industry, she was one of a group commandeered and converted for anti-submarine escort service. Fortunately she had never killed a whale and so was free of the stench of whale-oil which, once it pervades a ship, never leaves her.

As an oil-burner she was easier to keep clean than the coal-burning trawlers. She had a couple of knots more speed, and a rudder like a barn-door which made her extremely manoeuvrable. Against this was her low freeboard amidships, necessary for the towing of whale carcasses, two on either side. As a result, she was a semi-submarine in heavy weather, as I soon discovered. At those times the only way from the bridge to my cabin aft was along the top of the engine-room casing. She and her sister had been named after the enchanting stretches of water, beloved by poets and artists, of the English Lake District. They included *Buttermere* (our sister ship), *Ullswater, Thirlmere* and *Windermere.* Wastwater[1], remote and romantic, is the wildest and deepest lake in England.

However, not everyone responded to the magic. A US Navy sailor standing on the quay looked down, read the name, and exclaimed, "*Waste-water*! Gee, that's a hell of a name!"

The vessel in which, as it turned out, we were to circumnavigate the Atlantic, was 150 feet long, 50 feet longer than Cook's *Endeavour,* but with the same beam of 26 feet. She was 57 feet longer than Columbus's *Santa Maria.* Beside the towering sides of Nelson's 300-foot *Victory* she would have looked like a pinnace.

Living arrangements, I discovered, were even more congested and un-naval than in my previous trawlers: the naval principle of a separate living space for each category was out of the question in our case. Our small wardroom was next to the cook's galley which, as in all small ships, was the unofficial ship's club and gossip centre. The Captain's cabin, above the wardroom, was reached through the wireless cabin — the resort of signalmen and wireless operator. Our two small officers' cabins aft shared a companion ladder with the Petty Officers' mess, whence every sound was audible if not in fact amplified. Finally, with bridge and wheelhouse combined in one, the officer of the watch always had with him on the bridge the helmsman, the Asdic operator, the two lookouts and the signalman. Olympian aloofness and the practice of solitude were not catered for. The lack of privacy is, in varying degrees, characteristic of all small ships; but even so, *Wastwater* was an extreme case. "Cheek by jowl?" said Jones, the Sub. "It's living cheek by heel I object to." As he slept on the wardroom settee at sea, he frequently opened his eyes to find the Captain's boot or mine a few inches from his nose, as we propped ourselves against the roll of the ship and coped with breakfast.

As an Australian I never ceased to wonder at the human varieties represented in the small islands of Britain. Our com-

---

[1] (pronounced Wostwater — "o" as in "cost")

pany's origins ranged from the Hebrides to East Anglia, from Hull ("ooll") to Milford Haven. There were two Irish stokers from Liverpool. The variety of speech was matched by the variety of background: trawler-hand, merchant seaman, baker, brickmaker, tramdriver. There was even a concrete-mixer who in emergency did duty for the cook. His porridge was noteworthy.

I soon discovered that the hottest messdeck arguments hinged on local rivalries, the Red Rose and the White, the Leek and the Thistle. This variety was to prove a real asset in our long wanderings together. *Wastwater's* crew seemed gifted with an endless capacity for getting amusement out of one another's peculiarities: time and again an anxious situation or a boring and tedious job ended in hilarity and a story repeated round the messes and long remembered with relish.

I had one clear impression. *Wastwater's* company was a crowd of cheerful individualists. I had seen from the start that my job would consist not so much in flogging unwilling horses as in persuading the more willing ones to pull with the team.

There was the Asdic operator who did his monotonous job well, but who upon picking up a suspicious sound disdained the mechanical formula of "Echo bearing so-and-so", preferring the more conversational opening, "Any rocks around here, Sir?" Even Chief had a tendency to wrestle personally with a recalcitrant oil drum instead of directing a couple of his brawny stokers to the job. And there was Bunts, the signalman, who having taken down a dictated signal would con it over and reword any passage which he found a trifle obscure. Such collaboration was a little too enthusiastic. But it was an error on the right side.

In *Gavotte,* my job as First Lieutenant had been made easy by Pitt, the non-pareil of Cox'ns, who never brought a problem without a shrewd suggested solution, and had the crew in the hollow of his hand. Now I would need to be more personally decisive.

Each morning at 8.30 I met Leading-Seaman John Morrison to discuss work for the day. Morrison came from the Hebrides and claimed descent from survivors of the Spanish Armada wrecked on Scotland's west coast in 1588. His splicing and seamanship were accomplished, but he had a strain of gentle pessimism that I decided was not policy but constitutional.

"I want to get on with painting on deck today, Morrison."

"Aye, aye, Sir, but I don't think it's any use painting today, Sir."

"Why not?"

"We've only that dark grey in the store, Sir. It's not the right shade."

"Mmm ... well, we could paint inside the bulwarks, where the colour won't show much, and under the gun platform."

"Aye, we could do that, Sir. But paint's so poor these days, it's hardly worth it, Sir — it will soon have to be done again."

"All the more reason to paint as often as we can."

"Very good, Sir, but it won't last a month. And I doubt we may get some rain this morning to spoil it all."

Sometimes Morrison was right, and I would be wise to accept his recommendation. There is nothing like wasted effort to make unwilling workers. But it was part of my job to keep a wary eye open for the specious reason for not doing something.

Soon, authority was subjected to another sort of test. Griffith, a cheerful, plausible Welsh stoker, requested permission to report to the Sick Bay in the Base ship, and returned with a note from the Medical Officer to say that, owing to a slight knee injury, he should be put on Light Duty and especially should rest his knee.

"What do you think of it, Number One?" asked the Captain as he studied the MO's letter.

"Don't know, Sir. He was kicking a football about yesterday. May be a genuine case, though."

"Well, we'll soon find out."

It was really quite simple. The Navy, in dealing with generations of ingenious scrimshankers, has evolved an answer to almost every such situation, in this case the simple formula that men who are sick are debarred from being granted shore leave. It happened to be our first day alongside in the harbour, when access to the cinemas and canteens was pleasantly easy.

"Rest must be the keynote," said the Captain. "He must turn into his bunk at once and stay there. Doctor's orders and mine."

On receipt of these instructions, the invalid's face lengthened. "Oh, my knee's not really that bad, Sir. I can walk on it all right; I can get along all right ashore, Sir."

"No, the Captain has a letter from the MO and you are to turn in immediately. You must try rest, complete rest, to get that knee better."

That evening on our way ashore the Captain and I visited the sick man in his bunk. Returning from the cinema we again paid an official visit to the thoroughly bored patient, spoke a few words of sympathy and inspected the knee.

Early next morning I heard brisk steps descending the companion ladder. It was Stoker Griffith, his usual cheerful self.

"Good morning, Sir. The Chief's sending me over for some stores this morning."

"Right. Carry on, Griffith."

"And about my knee, Sir — "

"Yes?"

"You'll be pleased to hear, Sir, that it's completely cured, Sir."

The next issue involved our need, as one of HM Ships (as genuinely "White Ensign" as any battleship) to "play Navies" now and again. The Captain was turning over the morning's crop of correspondence and signals.

"Oh, look here, did you see this one? We've got to send a party of six hands to a Naval Funeral this afternoon. 'Fraid there's no help for it. Anyway, it won't do some of 'em any harm to look smart and Naval once in a while. Send a couple of the fishermen in the party."

Accordingly, the party of six whom I detailed to fall in on the quay in their best Number Two uniforms at 1400 that afternoon included two of our "Grimmies". Now, this parading business touched a very deep-seated prejudice in the trawlermen's philosophy. They were, and knew it, among the best seamen we had. Our present life was not so far removed from their peacetime experience. Their idea in joining the Navy was to beat the lights out of Jerry and then get back to fishing. They were rough, tough trawlermen and didn't go much on this Navy routine, just a lot of **** polish to no **** purpose. Funeral Parties an' all.

Seaman Ribble was spokesman; he had a request to see the Captain.

"Well?"

"Request to see the Captain to be excused from Funeral Party."

"For what reason?"

Some glitter in the Captain's eye seemed to convey a warning to the champion of self-determination. He had not expected much trouble in evading the tiresome duty. He shifted his feet.

"Well, Sir, it's seein' 'as 'ow I 'aven't got a decent Number Two uniform, not decent like, to wear to a funeral."

The Captain paused. "The Funeral Party will be inspected by the First Lieutenant at a quarter to two. If you, Ribble or any of the others have not a decent uniform then, your leave will be stopped for a fortnight, or until you have a decent uniform. If your uniform isn't good enough for a Funeral Party it certainly isn't good enough to go ashore in."

The Funeral Party from HMS *Wastwater* fell in at 1400, all present and correct. Said the Captain, who attended the service and marched all the way with them, "I must say our fellows were the smartest of the lot".

COs are liable to a certain fosterparental pride.

At times compromise was required. The Captain found a thread of blue wool in his coffee cup. "I don't much like the idea of dirty socks in the sink where our wardroom cups are washed," he remarked. "You might grind out some orders to that effect." So I duly drafted and published orders that in future galley sinks were not to be used for dobeying, as this practice was unhygienic, etc. Immediately arose a cry of lamentation and protest.

Where else could the dobeying of clothes be done? Reply: in buckets. But a bucket was not capacious enough. In the portable tin wash-tub then. Ah. But what was one among so many?

Besides, the hot water must then be conveyed from the engine room. What about dobeying in the engine room tunnel then? But here the Chief rightly protested against such an invasion. And then (the final shot), why should a time-honoured procedure be changed? Ever since *Wastwater* was first at sea, dobeying had been done in the galley sinks: to withdraw the privilege would render life intolerable. The last reason was the truest, for the seaman is indeed a creature of habit. Chalmers, late of Glasgow Tramways Union, was the most fluent spokesman for popular rights.

At last, after investigation and report by a committee consisting of the Coxswain, myself and advisers, a suitable compromise was decided on. whereby one of the two sinks was set aside for dobeying, the other reserved for dish-washing only. Order signed and posted. Resumption of the normal services. Thus tradition and progress were reconciled. But the Captain still nervously examined his cup for any trace of seaboot stocking, despite the steward's assurances.

Those evenings at anchor were an unusual chance for the three of us in *Wastwater*'s wardroom to talk at leisure. After supper was cleared away and the doors jammed against galley noises on one side and the Arctic night on the other, we could settle down to compare our varied experiences before fate or accident brought us together.

The Captain, John May, was 42 to my 26 and Jones' 25. A pipe-smoking, mild-mannered Londoner who relished company and conversation, his experience of the sea and of civilian life far outstripped mine. He had spent eight years in the Merchant Navy, acquiring a Second Mate's ticket and then had worked for a publishing firm. (This latter experience proved a boon to me later when we found ourselves in New York.) He had a wife and a two-year-old son in England and was proud of his father ("my old man"), the writer and Catholic convert J. Lewis May. Joining the RNVR, he had spent the early part of the war as a Boarding Officer in a trawler on the notoriously gruelling Northern Patrol, for which he had been awarded an OBE, and had then been appointed First Lieutenant of *Buttermere*. *Wastwater* was his first command. His rank, like mine, was Lieutenant, but he could soon expect his extra half stripe to Lieutenant Commander. He was modest about his achievements, averse to standing on his dignity as Captain and ready to take his full share in our more humdrum duties. With only three of us, that was going to make all the difference.

Sub-Lieutenant Geoffrey Jones was an irrepressible Lancastrian, whose effervescent wit cheered us in many a trying situation. He was our universal man-for-all-seasons. Whatever new thing was to be coped with, Jones would cope. He united the functions of Gunnery Officer, Navigating Officer and Wardroom Secretary, and in each achieved a frivolous efficiency which was worth a lot. Early in the war, when he was a signalman, his cruiser had been mined in the Channel: he had been thrown from his bunk into total darkness and was one of the lucky survivors. He wore the blue and white ribbon of the Distinguished Service Medal, having volunteered for a party dismantling a new type of German magnetic mine on a drifter in the middle of Scapa Flow. Jones claimed to have joined the party in error, having heard some remark about "free beer", but the story deceived no one. Soon afterward he received his commission and was appointed to *Wastwater*.

He was our wardroom authority on the Navy. As an RNVR rating in peacetime he had seen the Navy before its invasion by the tide of amateurs. As signalman in his cruiser he knew most of what went on. In him I observed the advantage of a commission through the lower deck (which my brother Peter, enlisting later than me, likewise had).

Jones' experience gave him just the right blend of sympathy and realism in his dealing with the hands. Happily we were not much troubled in *Wastwater* by the old sea-lawyer, with his snippets of King's Regulations and Admiralty Instructions. But if we had been, Jones knew all the answers. He was not married, but had a girl in Liverpool. Before the war he had been employed in a Liverpool hat shop. He initiated us into the arts by which a customer could be made uncomfortable until he had bought a new hat. By the time we reached New York, Jones had revealed yet another talent, a flair for humorous verse in the style of Stanley Holloway's *Albert and the Lion*.

I quickly became convinced that we were going to have a congenial wardroom, the most important start towards having a happy ship. The evening would wear away as we sat exchanging stories. We took for granted the ultimate "final victory" promised by Churchill, but it still looked a long way off and speculation was pointless: we had plenty to do and our immediate small world was demanding enough. At last Jones would get up and brew us a nightcap of hot whisky or cocoa; and with yawning good nights we would step out from the bright warmth of the wardroom to the open deck and a wind blowing icy off the white mountains, and the dark shapes of the ships on the anchorage, and the clustered lights of Reykjavik, and the water slapping along the side as we rode easily at anchor.

CHAPTER 8

ARCTIC CIRCLE

We had a variety of weather in those winter months in Iceland, ranging from bad, through very bad, to vile. The wind too varied, from mere strong to hurricane force. Once the arrow of the Aneroid barometer went right off the scale: "Chucked 'is 'and in, Sir," said Bunts, on noting the phenomenon. Our trips consisted mainly of escorting small convoys around the coasts, where the shallower water achieved a short steep sea in which *Wastwater*'s rolling and pitching were peculiarly vicious.

Coastal navigation is sometimes contemptuously referred to by deep-sea men as "point-to-point". It certainly requires less theoretical knowledge than finding your way over a featureless ocean by astronomical calculations; on the other hand the margin for error is appreciably smaller.

This is a filthy night: our first night out with a northbound convoy, creeping up the dangerous indented west coast. It is pitch black at 4 am when I relieve Jones, and it will be dark all my watch. I stick my head under the canvas flap of the chart table, and study the situation. "There's Helgi light flashing just abaft the beam," I hear Jones say. "I make us about two and a half miles off." Yes, that's it on the chart; that means we're just crossing one of those deep bays or fjords that gash this whole bit of coast. "Course north thirty east; we're making good about seven and a half knots."

I do some quick mental arithmetic. That means we should be seeing the light on the next headland in about half an hour. Right. I duck out of the bright chart table, and for a minute can see nothing. Where's the convoy? What? Oh, yes; no; yes, there's one dim shape, just discernible, and there's another: good enough. One-oh-one revs. Right 'o ... Jones is gone, and I am alone, in sole charge of the ship and all her company, as we plough through the night and the sea, which I feel and hear, but cannot separate from the general blackness.

First to get this sticky bridge window up another two inches.

I am taller than Jones, and my chin is freezing rapidly. I peer at the convoy through glasses, four ships now: my eyes are more accustomed to the dark, keeping station on the funnel of that big merchantman. This sea on the bow is the devil: better when we alter course. Swish, bang! I duck as a sheet of spray flies over the bridge. As we roll everything groans, and the parallel rulers race across the chart table with a maddening whirr.

Only another four hours of this. I begin to dream of the ecstasy of going below at eight: thank heaven the Coxswain is punctual in relieving. I come back to find the helmsman eight degrees off his course: "Watch it, now!" We can't afford to wander here. Wonder if this wind and sea are setting us inshore much?

I check the echo-sounder. Well, plenty of water under us: but it's deep water right to the cliffs here. Wonder if I could see that light yet: Skullness or Skaldurness? No, not a thing visible.

Time? Four-twenty. Bit early yet I suppose. At four twenty-five I think I see a dim flicker right ahead. If so we'll have to alter course to seaward. Wonder if I should alter course, in case? Don't want to get too near the convoy, though, in this weather.

"Lookout, keep your eyes skinned for a flashing light ahead." Four-thirty now: really should be seeing it. A spasm of doubt grips me about the course. Check it quickly: no, all's well there.

Unpleasant coast to run up on, this. Not much chance really if you did, with water this temperature anyway. Remember that trawler in the Hebrides ... Down forrard in the messes the men off watch are sleeping like the dead — supreme confidence, supreme indifference — whichever you like. Navigation is someone else's job: mine, in fact.

Should I call the Captain? Nearly four-forty now. We must see that light: visible eight miles, according to the chart. What if by some ghastly mischance it were extinguished, and not only we, but the whole convoy ... Yes, I must call the Captain: one quick sweep with the glasses first, though, and then in the mingled blackness of sky and sea a tiny tongue of light licks. We're all right. Relief floods over me. There's even time to send down for a cup of cocoa, and for a few shouted pleasantries with the helmsman. So far so good.

As the light moves from the bow to the beam I take bearings for a "running fix" of the ship's position. We learned this exercise in simple trigonometry during training at *King Alfred,* but a year at sea has not dulled the childish mixture of surprise and satisfaction it always gives me to find that it really works in practice.

"0450 Skaldurness abeam starb'd. 2.4 miles," I note in the Log Book. Already it is dropping astern, out of mind: already my thoughts are groping forward to our rendezvous with destiny, the end for which we strive, the real pinnacle of achievement, the Future ... Langdanes lighthouse.

These were days before the full weight of Jerry's air and U-boat attacks had developed against the Russian convoy route; but there were two sides to that. As the long hours of darkness and the fury of the weather made it more difficult for the U-boat packs and the bomber squadrons, so they increased the ever-present danger of collision, icebergs or foundering: ships were known to stray from the convoy into the Arctic gloom and never be heard of again. But whether the enemy were U-boat and Heinkel or the malevolent weather, where the convoys went the trawlers went with them, the makeshift escorts which, intended merely as temporary stop-gaps, still proved themselves indispensable. And the cargoes were desperately needed by the Russians, our allies since Hitler's blitzkrieg attack.

Our orders, however, were to leave the convoy 300 miles north of Iceland, and we weren't sorry.

Daylight lasted from 10 am to 3 pm and it was getting colder hourly. It was snowing hard too, a white curtain drifting ceaselessly between the black sky and the black engulfing water. As we turned away I caught a last glimpse of the heaving merchantmen disappearing into the desolate Northern gloom, steering for the North Cape. Then I went down to the cheerful brightness of the wardroom to enjoy a cup of hot tea and one of Jones' plausible stories.

The next day was our first experience of "icing-up", a major problem with all exposed gear in these latitudes. It snowed all night, and as each drop of the flung spray touched the ship it froze hard. When the sun broke through at eleven o'clock, we might have been a ship of sugar-icing. Mast, bridge, ventilators, everything dressed in frosty white: the standing rigging all picked out like the tinsel cord round Christmas parcels. But under the gun-platform forrard was the most miraculous change. The supporting stanchions were like pillars of salt, a foot thick, while from the edge and underside of the platform itself hung great conical stalactites, matching the humps and pinnacles growing up from the deck below. It might have been a stage setting for caves of ice in Xanadu. As I mentioned this thought to the Captain, the Chief's voice behind us struck a discordant but timely note.

"Reckon we'll 'ave to do summat about this bloody ice: it's increasin' top-weight, like."

The Chief was right: our rolling had increased perceptibly, which was not surprising with a foot of ice covering the whole upper deck. It would be dangerous if the sea rose much. The wan oblique sunlight wouldn't melt it in a month: there was only one thing for it. Without delay all available hands were armed with axes, shovels and crowbars and went to work, hacking, prodding, shovelling, chipping. There was a grotesque novelty in clambering over hummocks and under icicles on our own familiar deck. It was warm work.

Half-way through we paused to drink black tea and pose for photographic groups variously suggested as "The Russian Front" and "Amundsen at the Pole". Further light relief was supplied when a stoker, after twenty minutes battering at a peculiarly obstinate ice hummock, was discovered to be assaulting one of the mooring bollards. This incident provided material for mess-deck wit for several days.

Akureyri, where we fuelled, is the second town of Iceland, and generally considered more characteristically Icelandic than Reykjavik, the capital, which stands in the stream of foreign trade and external influences. Its five thousand inhabitants were largely occupied in their forbears' pursuits: fishing, the fur industry, the weaving of tweed, grazing and farming. Akureyri is the home of the famous Icelandic Blue cheese.

That passage from Akureyri to Reykjavik was the worst I had ever known. It disclosed potentialities for villainy in *Wastwater* beyond anything I had dreamed of. There were, of course, technical reasons which made it inevitable that in a short head-on sea she would pitch badly. But the extra viciousness and violence, the personal venom with which she banged, shuddered and hit you: that, I became convinced, could only be explained as calculated and intentional spite.

The one ray of light amid the general gloom was the hope of mail. It was six weeks since we had sailed from Aberdeen that rainy midnight, and we had had no mail in the interval. Surely bags of it must now be awaiting us in Reykjavik? That could atone for this present beastliness.

A few notes jotted at the time make it possible to distinguish day from night in what seemed one interminable nightmare.

> *Sunday.* 1300. Fair passage down Eija Fjord. 2000. Wind SW, Force 5, increasing. Glass falling. Ship rolling a bit but wind still offshore. Keeping station three cables astern of "Cape Casablanca". Intermittent rain squalls. Bunk the only tolerable place: turn in straight after my watch — Hatch still leaking — must get that fixed. Also lavatory door, which bangs infernally in the flat. At least my bunk is high and dry. Could mail really be waiting for us ahead?

> *Monday.* 4 am. Round the corner, steering SW wind hurricane force, W to SW. Steep short seas, the worst yet. Miserable watch. "Cape Casablanca" ahead, pounding heavily — seas breaking over her. She signals "Reduce to 8 knots". But seas still like battering rams.
> Come down to breakfast — find six inches of water swishing across after end of wardroom, Jones prostrate on settee. Nibble some baked beans, get down a few sips of coffee, doze in chair till "Rum Oh". Descend shakily to the

messdeck — a wet shambles, several new hands flaked right out. But most get their tots down.

A sepulchral voice mutters, "Always knew I should 'ave been a farmer". Battle with cook's raisin duff for lunch, while seas go roaring along the deck six feet away. We seem to be sitting right *in* the sea — is there any beginning or end to this?

1600. Relieve Jones on watch — wonder do I look like that? Feel like death. Hold out till 1700, then am sick like the rest. (Note: Raisin duff, to digest, four hours insufficient).

Tuesday. 0200. Anchor in Reykjavik Roads — still blowing, ship still rolling — but, by contrast, peace.

1000. Ashore for stores, etc. Learn that our mail has been wrongly directed back to Britain and won't be here for another week or ten days. Some unspeakable idiot should be keel-hauled.

In the afternoon we make our way to Hvalfjord, and go alongside the oiler. It seems easy after coaling. We simply secure alongside the great broody oil tanker — our bridge level with her upper deck — lower the huge hose which they pass us into our fuel tank and give the word to pump away. Like a patient taking pre-digested food through a rubber tube. I watch the Chief and his black gang securing the end of the pipe, while a chain of messengers is posted to pass instructions to the pumps on the oiler.

Alas, a vulture-like vigilance is necessary, and on this occasion is not forthcoming. There is a sudden frantic shouting of "stop poompin' on oiler" echoed and re-echoed along the line. Too late! The copious pipe is still full of oil, the black, pitchy flood pours over the tank-tops, spreading across my beautiful deck like a tide of lava. Someone lets go the end of the pipe. It flies out, spattering oil everywhere. I glimpse the Chief, wrestling with it like Laocoon, oil-bespattered, more lugubrious than ever. The shrill voice of the Gunner cries, "Oooooh look, Chief's got his tiddly suit on too!" Everyone is much cheered by this incident, except Chief, who somehow always seems to be wearing his smart "tiddly" uniform for such occasions; myself, to whom the prospect of oily boots clumping about the deck is not pleasing; and the stokers, who with bales of cotton waste and buckets of paraffin, set about cleaning up the mess.

Those were weeks of phenomenal gales even for Iceland. During one blow of 120 miles an hour the whole personnel of the RAF aerodrome had to be turned out in the middle of the night to man the wings of the grounded aircraft to prevent them being torn away to destruction; and some wit originated the famous signal, "One Nissen Hut airborne 0330 hrs. ETA 0335".

In such weather life for us was little more restful in harbour than at sea. Sometimes it was more perilous. That first night, after our trip from Akureyri, oiling completed, we got permission to stay alongside the oiler, lying at her permanent moorings. "We can get back to Reykjavik Roads as soon as it's light," said the Captain. "The glass is still low, but the wind's gone down a lot. What a lousy trip that was. I feel absolutely done in."

Just after 10 o'clock, before turning in, I stepped out on deck. The wind had almost died away, and some stars were visible overhead. It was bitterly cold, and the mountain walls of Hvalfjord loomed colossal. But we seemed snug and secure enough nestling alongside the tanker.

"Call me if it blows up, quartermaster; otherwise, usual time."

"Aye, aye, Sir."

Oh, the bliss of changing into pyjamas and rolling into my comfortable bunk. Before switching off the reading lamp over my head I looked round my cabin: the white lockers, the medicine chest, the washbasin, the desk with Honor's photograph, the small bookshelf, so apt to fling its contents over me if not carefully wedged. It was so snug and secure and gave me the feeling that whatever happened in the world outside, though the ship as a whole should meet with several kinds of disaster, my small cabin would remain safe and unaffected. It was a bad case of ostrichism.

It was at 1.20 am that the quartermaster called me. It was Holtby, his usual polite self.

"First Lieutenant, Sir."

"Yes, what is it?"

"I thought I should tell you, Sir."

"Tell me what?"

"The wires, Sir, they've parted fore and aft, we're adrift."

Cursing and hitting things I pull on boots and a coat and stumble on deck, colliding with Jones and the Captain on their way up to the bridge.

"Shall I stand by the anchor?" I bellow in the Captain's ear.

"Yes, will you? No use trying to get alongside the tanker again. Let me know if the anchor holds."

Up forrard the fo'c's'le party are waiting, crouched over the windlass, exposed to the full force of the driving horizontal sleet which strikes your face and hands like red hot needles.

"Anchors cleared away Morrison?"

"Aye, aye, Sir, all ready for letting go."

We can only communicate by shouting with cupped hands, and not a word can be heard from the bridge. I dodge back and climb up to the bridge and report all ready.

"All right, we'll let go four shackles in a minute. We're too close to the oiler yet."

Jones is under the chart table flap, studying the chart of the anchorage. It is not a pleasant situation. The hurricane had burst at a quarter past one, coming down the mountain walls of the fjord like a thunderbolt, parting wires and moorings, sinking boats, smiting ships, blotting everything out with a furious sleet. Every ship in the fjord was dragging her anchor, and even the tanker tugged savagely at the great chains of her permanent moorings. Our mooring ropes which secured us alongside her strained and parted in quick succession; and now she was disappearing fast into the rain and gloom as we drifted away, beam on before the blizzard.

"Can't go far this way," shouted Jones from the chart table. "About three cables to those rock ledges."

"Let go starboard anchor."

I stumble forrard and sign to let go. As the anchor runs out I note that the usually deafening clatter of the chain cable is inaudible in this greater tumult. Two shackles, three shackles, four shackles.

"Hold on." The cable comes taut a moment, then sags, then taut. We're dragging the anchor along the sea bottom.

"Give her another shackle." But the cable jumps as before, and the wind is still on our beam.

"She's not holding an inch," cries one of our veteran fishermen.

To every one of us comes the thought, how much further, how much longer? I report again to the bridge: "Anchor dragging".

"All right, we're steaming half ahead, hard a-starboard. Watch the cable".

Then suddenly the cable shifts from right abeam to the bow, and we are coming round, heading up into the wind. Praise be for *Wastwater*'s handiness! For the moment we have checked the drift.

Only then do we realise that we are frozen. Never before had I felt cold as such a physical pain. But not a man moved to shelter or for warmer clothes till I said, "All right, fall out, but stand by ready". We had all forgotten our personal misery in our determination to make that anchor hold.

It was the worst night of my life. Hour after hour the hurricane blew with undiminished force. We could see nothing fixed but the dim lights of the tanker: so we kept our bearing on her, and mercifully her moorings held. All through that fiendish night lights kept appearing, changing, disappearing, as ships all round us dragged, weighed anchor, steamed round, anchored again, between the double peril of collision and running up on the rockbound shore.

All the time we kept steaming half ahead, taking the strain off the cable, up ten revolutions if we seemed to be dropping astern, down ten as we seemed to be overrunning the cable, and praying all the time for daylight and the wind to ease.

At nine o'clock it got light, and the wind dropped as suddenly as it came. Ships were strewn round the anchorage in confusion, some with fouled anchors, some in the berths of others, one or two with scars of collisions. On a sharp pinnacle of rock half a mile away a small merchant ship was perched, bridge half-way up, funnel leaning drunkenly back. It looked as though a small push would be sufficient to take her right over the top and send her slithering down the other side. We learned later that three other ships in the more exposed roadstead at Reykjavik had dragged up onto a reef and broken up. The majority of their crews got ashore on a breeches buoy, but some slipped into the sea and were lost.

So much for our quiet night in.

CHAPTER 9

CHRISTMAS IN ICELAND

On Christmas Day, five weeks after we had left home, it snowed and we were still without mail. Then it was that I discovered a whole new respect for the resourcefulness and resilience of our motley crew.

On Christmas Eve, we had just finished supper in the wardroom when there was a shuffling on deck, the flicker of a lantern — the emergency anchor light, I noted — and a raucous chorus struck up "Good King Wenceslas". Our invitation to "come in and have one" was not spurned. Led by Morrison, the minstrels stood round studying their glasses with as much nudging and giggling as any waits.

On Christmas morning we had a short service in the messdeck, with the prayer for absent families and friends read by the Captain. The messdeck was festive with paper bells and streamers bought from mess funds, and for Christmas dinner the cook had excelled himself. We had roast chicken (in lieu of turkey) with roast potatoes and peas which had once been green, mince pies (the cook had a skilled hand with pastry) and a plum pudding containing all the fruits of the Orient and half a bottle of sherry. In accordance with naval custom, we three officers were messmen for the day. I saw the Captain, clutching a dish of roast potatoes, slide from top to bottom of the companion ladder without touching a single rung, while Jones washed up the dirty plates in a somewhat greasy mess bucket. I was dishing up, and witty comments were not lacking if the messman seemed slow or double-thumbed.

When even the hungriest stoker was replete, glasses were filled, "marcella whiffs" lighted, and a small sing-song began. Mouth organs appeared, old favourites were roared, soloists were called for. Stoker Bird gave his rendering of "Pennies from Heaven" (amended to "Kronur" to give local colour) and the Chief sang (an annual event). The song was inaudible, but we could see the Chief's foot beating time, and a general sense of rhythm pervaded the messdeck. Presently the level of the entertainment,

which had started with "Nowell" and some carols, began to
decline. Glances were passed round, the officers were eyed to see
how we would take it; calls for a well-known bawdy ditty began
to be heard. Then a surprising thing happened. Eighteen-year-old
Guns, our youngest seaman, who got ragged a good deal by the
others, called out from a corner, blushing the while, "Come on
now, lads ye've all the year for that. This is Christmas Day". The
current was deflected. With some more songs and recitations (not
of the kind suggested) we dispersed, to sleep or write letters. I felt
a ballad was called for.

Christmas in Iceland

We lay in Iceland winterbound,
And heard the blizzard blow,
And naught we saw on sea or shore
Except the driving snow.

Then said our Captain to the Cook,
At anchor as we lay,
"Make us a duff with all your might;
Tomorrow's Christmas Day!"

Then said the Cook, "A Scotsman I,
My season's Hogmanay,
Yet will I make a mighty duff
To eat on Christmas Day".

On Christmas Day it still snowed on,
No news from home had we,
But we'd the Cook's great Christmas duff,
And our good company.

The wind blew wild, the snow it piled
On decks your boot would freeze on,
But in the mess-deck down below
We kept the Christmas season.

With paper streamers all was rigged,
The officers were messmen,
Of seaman, stokers, bunts and all,
None greater were nor less men.

And there was light and warmth and cheer,
No plate nor glass stood empty,
A genial glow lit every heart
Of all our eight and twenty.

We sang the songs we'd sung at home
In Christmases gone by:
Till some for bawdy choruses
Began to call and cry.

Then spoke our youthful gunner, and
With furious blush cried "Nay!
Ye've all the year for that my lads;
But this is Christmas Day".

Another growled, "Why rot we here?
A dog's a better life —
Never to see my bairns, nor sleep
Beside my wedded wife".

But Coxswain answered, clenching pipe,
"I've wife and kids as well,
But I'd fight the sea and the enemy
From Iceland on to Hell,

So be I knew they'd not lose heart,
Though home I never come,
Till they and all true-hearted folk
Have Christmas safe at home".

So it was done and said and sung,
And our thoughts went homeward winging

Over the long black ocean leagues,
And a quietness followed the singing,

And aloft the snow picked out each spar,
Each stay and bolt and splicing,
And our good ship rode in the Arctic night
Like a ship of sugar-icing.

We saw the New Year in on patrol. A note of tragedy was struck by the episode of the cook. Conscientious to a degree, and at other times strictly abstemious, he nevertheless felt that a stern obligation lay upon him, as a loyal Glasgow Scot, to get royally drunk on Hogmanay. He told his plans to the steward, and it became common talk of the ship that Cookie would be out of action on Hogmanay night. There was something impressive in so cold-blooded and thorough a preparation.

When he found we were to pass our New Year at sea, he was disconsolate in the extreme. However, after consultation with several fellow Scots on board, it was adjudged that the correct rite might safely be celebrated a day or two late without prejudice to its efficacy.

On our first night in harbour, Cookie and his pal the steward girded themselves and set off ashore with grim purposeful determination. To their utter dismay, they discovered that the inflexible ration at the wet canteen was one bottle of beer per man per night. Within an hour they were back on board, both as sober as judges, and bitterly disillusioned patriots.

"I'm tellin' ye," exclaimed the cook, "it's yon sort of thing drives men to drink."

In the wardroom, we held deferred celebrations of the New Year in the form of a modest lunch party, one of our guests being Williams, secretary to the British Legation, and a school friend of the Captain's. We little guessed when, where, and under what circumstance he would again be our guest in *Wastwater*.

71

CHAPTER 10

FROM FISH TO THE FLEET

As a converted whaler, *Wastwater* enjoyed a unique position in nautical society: we liked to think we were at home in any company.

One day in the harbour we berthed outside a Grimsby fishing trawler, just in. Several of our "Grimmies" immediately boarded the trawler for news of their home town, and returned with a gift of fish sufficient to make several meals for the whole ship. In the evening we invited the two skippers to our wardroom for a drink. They were elderly (the young men had all been called up), apple-cheeked, and twinkling — perfect fishermen of fiction or the advertisements. They rolled their own cigarettes of black shag, and their talk mingled simplicity with shrewd humour. One of them told us of his adventures in a remote Icelandic hospital, where they took his temperature in a place he wasn't used to, and how he got out by removing the thermometer when the nurse was out of the room and shaking it vigorously down.

For their part, these hale old Grimsby skippers were surprised to find the likes of us living in the ships they were bred to, navigating them about the ocean, meeting the same dangers and discomforts. Warm with good cheer, their own eloquence, and our Johnny Walker, they climbed back aboard their trawler.

The next afternoon, as we were getting ready to go to Hvalfjord for oil, we received a request from the Naval Stores Officer.

"They ask if we will take twenty bags of coke to the cruiser *Cumberland*, said the Captain. "Missed the routine store boat."

"Somewhat undignified job for an HM ship," I objected. "Make a mess of the deck too."

"Oh, well, it's on our way," said the Captain, who was always inclined to stretch a point to do anyone a favour.

We took the coke and in due course went alongside the *Cumberland* to deliver it.

In the dusk our ensign would be hard to make out, and our

lines were not exactly naval, so that possibly their Officer of the Watch did not realise that we were an HM ship. Such an error on the part of a Big Ship Man would not have surprised us.

As we slid alongside, our bridge just level with the cruiser's deck, I looked up at the formidable turrets, and felt the jar of solid armour-plating against our side. Presently a huge crane, large enough to lift *Wastwater,* coke and all, onto her deck, swung over us, the bags were rolled into an enormous wire net, a well-bred voice began to chant, "Lower — purchase — hoist — purchase — handsomely," and the coke went swaying up into the darkness above our heads and out of our ken.

Wastwater was lying snugly enough alongside her big sister, and our request to remain there for the night brought an "Approved" and an invitation to visit. So while some of our hands attended the *Cumberland*'s cinema, the Captain, Jones and I donned more respectable uniform and climbed aboard to pay a social call.

The cruiser seemed immense, invincible, a creature of a different world. The great guns and the spacious quarterdeck and wardroom-flat aroused our envious admiration. At the same time we were on our mettle. I noted severely a bulkhead where the paintwork showed signs of neglect.

Our reception in the wardroom could not have been friendlier. As a small ship man, I had expected a more formal atmosphere in a cruiser's wardroom.

"You fellows from the — er — vessel alongside?" said an Engineer Commander. "What'll you have? By Jove, never imagined you'd be able to keep so clean and smart aboard there. Matter of fact I'm afraid I thought you were — er — "

"The coke boat?" said the Captain. "Sir, I must inform you that we belong to the Fifty-second A/S Striking Force."

We all laughed and relaxed from then on. The Captain's statement was strictly accurate. We had originally been organised with five other whalers as the Fifty-second Anti-submarine Striking Force, though not since Norway had the ships operated together.

Soon we were all deep in conversation, comparing notes and problems. I found myself bemoaning with the Commander the shortage of experienced senior ratings, and the foul weather in these parts which made painting the ship an impossibility. Common concerns jumped the gulf between his three straight stripes and my two wavy ones. When I mentioned that we were woefully short of paintbrushes he immediately sent down to the central store and presented me with a dozen, waving away the punctilious supply-rating who wanted me to sign a demand note for them. Oddly, our two ships had, in different ways, the same job to do, guarding the convoy routes in all weathers.

"The worst *I'd* ever seen," the Engineer Commander was saying. "One of the other cruisers had a gun turret torn clean off. It's the first time I've been up on our bridge — you've seen its height — and looked *up* at the waves. We lost boats, smashed up a lot of gear on deck. Everything else had gone back to harbour, destroyers and so on. Except the trawlers. Just us and the trawlers left at sea."

We felt a spurt of pride, but passed it off casually. We could sense these Big Ship men looking down at *Wastwater* and thinking, "Hm, wonder how I'd get on at sea in a thing like *that*".

Soon after our arrival in Reykjavik we heard of the Japanese attack on Pearl Harbour. We could get the BBC Home Service on the ship's set and a little knot of men used to gather round the door of the wireless cabin while "Sparks" tuned in to the six o'clock news. Somehow it helped to remind us that there *was* such a place as Britain, where folk we knew were listening to those same modulated tones at that very moment. Also it was the time when the Luftwaffe were making "sharp attacks" against "east coast towns". Our men from Hull, Grimsby and Aberdeen heard the formula in anxious silence.

I had missed the news that day for some reason, and put my head inside the door of the wireless cabin to enquire if there was anything special. Sparks looked round, "Oh, aye, Sir; there was an attack on a south-east coast town last night, two raiders shot down. And the Japs have bombed the American base at Pearl Harbour".

Over supper we discussed the news. Well, the American people wouldn't need to debate any more whether they should join in "the shooting war": it had been decided for them. Good thing for us, undoubtedly: should help a lot to clear the air. The Japs had asked for trouble and no doubt they would get it.

My thoughts went to Australia, and how they would be taking it out there. The Japanese menace had been a bogey as long as I could remember, but Japan was four thousand sea miles from Melbourne, and my father had spoken of the Singapore Base as Australia's front line of defence.

Meanwhile there were more immediate domestic matters. Where did the Captain think we should stow the new towing spring? Casually we left the subject, little guessing its full significance in world history or its early and drastic repercussions on the lives of each one of us in *Wastwater*.

CHAPTER 11

FIRST MAIL

At last mail had come — seven fat sacks of it — our first since leaving home nearly two months before.

We poured it all out — letters, parcels, papers and all — on the wardroom table and began sorting: Seamen's mess, Stokers' mess, POs', Wardroom. I stole hungry glances at my growing heap of letters, but not till the last sack had been carefully shaken and the last pile despatched to the messes was I able to carry them off to my cabin and open them. A silence brooded over the ship, each man engrossed in his own news, and by an unwritten agreement, everything but the bare essentials had to wait until the mail had been read.

I put on one side the three or four papers, the official-looking envelope, the large package with Australian stamps on it, and opened Honor's letters, skimming the latest ones first to make sure all was well, and then beginning at the beginning.

The first two had been written from Aberdeen soon after we sailed. In a moment Iceland and the blizzard and miseries of the last weeks melted away and I was back there, across the thousand miles of North Atlantic, in another world.

It will be a week tomorrow since you went. The feeling I have at the moment is the inexorableness of the time before I see you again. I've just got to go through it. No matter how much I demand to be with you again it won't make the smallest difference to the ordering of HM ships. I can't take a train or charter an aeroplane — in fact there's nothing I can do. It's awfully good for me to be up against something that even a "determined chin" can't alter ...

To cheer me up, old David [the gardener] took me out to observe the bees having a little jaunt in the frosty after-noon sun ... On Thursday, I have to go to the Labour Exchange for an interview re calling up ...

Last night as I came up the hill I saw the Northern Lights for the first time — a clear green glow and static searchlight striking up towards the centre of the sky. There's a supernatural feeling about the silent spectacle — it seemed such a marvellous message somehow from that part of the world where you are ...

Had my interview at the Labour Exchange this morning. At first it all seemed very official, but the woman turned out to be such a nice understanding person, and seemed interested in me. She asked if I had any children and I told her about losing Robert. At the end she said, "I suppose you will be available to be called upon". I told her I was afraid not as I was expecting another baby. She said, "I do hope you have better luck this time, and take care of yourself".

... Had lunch in a cafe and got talking to a dear old thing, looked about 80, told me all about her "boys". She has seven children, all in war jobs or Services, all over the country; she's alone for the first time in her life. She's certainly made *her* contribution to the war effort.

The next letters were from Cheshire, where she had moved to be with friends in the country.

It's much warmer here than the north, with a clear sky faintly blue. Feel awfully well, and they are seeing that I go gently here. How I live for the moment of seeing you with your son or daughter, whichever it is to be. It seems an unbelievable thought. And yet it keeps on happening to all sorts of people!

17 Dec. No more news from you since Saturday. Meanwhile the Japs are driving on with a vengeance — since the loss of the *Prince of Wales* and the *Repulse* — what a staggering blow that must have been — there seems nothing to stop them. It looks like being a very close shave if we are going to save Singapore. We do seem to have totally underestimated the Jap's efficiency and his oriental fanaticism. The Russians have some element of it, which has saved Moscow this winter. But somehow we seem back to a pre-Dunkirk

position on a worldwide scale — the shock may yet save us from the complacency and lethargy that has been creeping over the war effort, both here and in the USA.

Your idea of sending *four* pairs of silk stockings sounds too marvellous — they are precious as gold. With great gnawing of the heart-strings I gave that bottle of 4711 Eau de Cologne to Dilly for Christmas — hope you don't mind too much — all her Christmas parcels were lost at sea on their way from South Africa.

23 Dec. Our wedding anniversary, and the countryside is covered in new-fallen snow — I trudged down through it all to the village this morning — the lovely soft feathery stuff, just as I'd always imagined it at home from picture books of English Christmases. The wind has been blowing it about like sand but it doesn't sting your face in the same way ...

Today I was thinking of our honeymoon in Devon, and how even then we felt glad we were going back to take our part in the struggle; and I was thanking God for the way we have been made so much a part of our generation. Everything we have had to do and suffer is so very much a part of our day and generation.

10th Jan. How I wish you could have shared the Christmas festivities here — the tree, the crib, the carol singing. I wondered very much where you were, and hoped you would be having it in harbour, preferably alongside some large ship!

I hear there have been terrific hurricanes in Iceland lately — thinking a lot about you and the ship, hoping you weren't at sea in them.

I will send the Nescafe if it can be got, which I doubt.

Do you realise it's over six weeks since you left — could we really be half-way to our next meeting, I wonder?

Your poems have come back again from the publisher, like the faithful dove with the usual olive branch in the shape of a kind word: they all talk of the paper shortage. My personal opinion is that they think the thing should be published with their better nature, but their carnal one won't take the risk. I'll try again ...

The Malaya calamity seems to be showing up a few rotten spots in the body politic ... what a ghastly mess. Darwin might be the next objective after Singapore. Our families have been much in my mind — their last letters gave a glimpse of just how serious things are looking in Australia. The Australian Government have sent appeals to London and Washington for reinforcements ... The Japs have certainly called our bluff ...

Feeling despondent the other day about the dawdling and complacency of the democracies, I suddenly realised that there was at least one democrat I could do something about. Darling, what a miracle it would be for me to become a disciplined person — even in things like getting up when the alarm goes, being punctual etc. But it will be all to the advantage of our future home: imagine lunch punctually at 1! ...

You are so much in my thoughts and prayers, you are never alone ...

Shutting my desk top, I went up on deck: the wet iron deck, the biting wind, the grey sea, the bleak inhospitable shore — it came over me like the cold touch of reality. This was our life, our world. "Our future home": but this was my home, this small floating steel box. The past was a dream, the future as thick and impenetrable as the cloud covering the head of Snaefelsjokull across the flow. A gust of rebellion swept over me: why should I be here, in this bleak anchorage, separated from wife and home and all that meant most to me? Why were we all here? What had the millions of British folk throughout the world wanted in 1939 except to live decently and at peace and to mind their own business? "We are so much a part of our generation," Honor had said. We had grown up, like our contemporaries, under the shadow of war, with horror and dread of it, hoping to the last moment that the catastrophe might yet be averted. I remembered my first emotion when the storm finally burst: despair for the future in general — but, uppermost, disgust at the frustration of my hopes and plans, at the ruin of my personal life.

I went forrard to find the others. The Captain had a pile of letters from his wife and his father, an author of note, who wrote regularly to him. "Listen to this," he said with a chuckle. "My old man writes: 'Since the raiding started again we don't get much sleep, and none of the doors or windows will shut properly. But there's one compensation for it — since then my constipation has given me no trouble whatever'. That's typical of him. You'd like my old man."

Jones had news that his brother in the Merchant Service had been at home for a week between trips, and that the girl he was engaged to had joined the Auxiliary Fire Service.

The Chief appeared in the doorway and began to relay bits of his own and others' news. The wife and kids had moved from Hull to get away from the bombing, gone to her mother in the country. Alf Holtby had a photo of his nipper: real lovely kid. Tom Chalmers' missus and several others were expecting to be called up soon for factory work. They'd all had to register. What a war, eh? No real bad news, anyway.

He drifted off. An extraordinary change had come over the whole ship. This morning Britain had seemed a world away; it might have been seven weeks or seven years since we left. Now every man's thoughts focused on some spot in those small islands. What we did here and our being here at all in this foreign anchorage only had meaning because of *them*: we ourselves were a small floating Britain, absent, for the time being, from our parent ship but insufficient of ourselves.

"A part of our generation." Separation and anxiety and hardship were the common lot these days. A pang of fear for Honor, and for the child we were to have, shot through me. But we had no more to bear than most, much less than many. With any luck I should be at home this time anyway.

Somehow the coming of the mail seemed to have focused the

picture of Britain more clearly than I had ever seen it: the picture of a quiet, decent, peaceable people, capable of great energy in the heat of crisis, of humorous heroism in moments of danger, but asking for no heroic role or great destiny, merely the chance to live out their own lives in peace.

A sober, decent ideal, worth fighting for. But was it enough? Was it possible? I thought of Australia and the catastrophic events of the last few weeks in the Pacific. Was it really the beginning of the dissolution of the British Empire? And would the world be any worse off if it were? Did we deserve to survive? I had no certain answers to the questions.

CHAPTER 12

THE ICELANDERS

During our limited expeditions ashore in Reykjavik, we discovered that the Icelanders disliked being associated with the North Pole.

The name Iceland is deceptive. Only a tiny fraction of the northern coast lies within the Arctic Circle, and the southern parts, warmed by the genial current of the Gulf Stream, have nothing like the extreme cold of central Canada or Siberia. In summer it is grassy and mild; in winter windswept and bleak, but Polar, no. The choice of a woven Polar Bear as the shoulder emblem for the British forces in Iceland gave the Icelanders some quiet amusement.

I heard an Icelandic journalist describe a tour of Britain. "Our first day being a Sunday," he said, "I of course seized the opportunity to visit Whipsnade Zoo in search of my old friend the Polar Bear. As these animals are not found in my own country, it was naturally a great experience to visit a land where they may be seen."

As we trudged the streets of Reykjavik, most of them unpaved — there were no trains or trams — it seemed a blend of frontier-town and provincial capital. Yet with its population of fifteen thousand, the abundance of book shops with publications in English and German being almost as common as those in Icelandic, was striking.

Oddly enough, my first personal introductions came from Australia and from academic links. At Melbourne University my friend and contemporary, Manning Clark, had plighted his troth with Dymphna Lodewyckx, daughter of the Professor of Germanic Languages, who had also been Honor's professor in her German studies. Manning and Dymphna, like Honor and me, had travelled to Europe and had been married in Oxford as war loomed. The Professor, an Icelandic enthusiast, had spoken to me of Iceland and now sent me some names, explaining, with war-time discretion, "In case you should be in that part of the world".

As a result, one bitter afternoon, I found myself standing in the snow knocking timidly at the door of a house on the outskirts of Reykjavik. Professor Nordal, whom I knew to be an authority on Icelandic literature, was cordiality itself: "Come in. And how is Professor Lodewyckx? He made so many friends here."

As his wife poured tea for us in the modest sitting room, he spoke warmly of the time he had spent at Oxford years before, and declared, "The British are the great administrators. They have had experience of it all over the world, and have learned so much from their mistakes". I thought of the contemporary scene — Malaya lost, Burma crumbling, India in ferment, Australian confidence shaken to the roots, and the to-and-fro battle for the Atlantic — and hoped he was right.

We invited him to visit us on board. He came with his two sons, one of whom "fostered" the RAF, the other the Royal Navy. Chief took them off to the engine room and gave his popular performance on the reversing engine. He was the kindest of men and loved to entertain. The Professor wedged himself into the wardroom settee.

"Time has come to Iceland during my life" he said. "When I was a boy we rode away to school on ponies, and a day here or there, it did not matter much. Now the wireless and the motor bus have brought Time — that is something new for us."

I mentioned the prosperity which the American and British occupation had brought to Iceland. "Yes, it has transformed our life," he said, "but will it last? Will it not be worse afterwards? That is what many of us fear." He went on to speak of his misgivings for the future of his country, of the restlessness of the young people, of his fear that the best traditions of Iceland would be submerged under a deluge of slick superficial Anglo-American culture. As he left, he gave me the name of a friend and colleague whom I might like to meet.

Professor Gudmansson shook my hand warmly when we met and immediately began conducting me over the modern university buildings. "From Australia? Yes I remember our friend Lodewyckx. He was very much liked here. Here is our History School, there is our Theology School, here is the Biology Laboratory, and here the Chemistry and Science." He showed me the light and beautiful Chapel, the comfortable common-rooms of professors and students. I asked if there were a residential college.

"Ah, there you see it!" He pointed through the window to a building some distance away. "But now you have it for your hospital, alas!" He beamed and shook his head. I said I was sorry that the necessities of war had caused the occupation and some hardships. Had there been any trouble between our troops and the Icelanders perhaps? "No, no," he protested, "Your British soldiers, they have behaved themselves very well, oh, very well indeed." Beaming, he reverted to Latin to sum up his view of the situation. "You, and now the Americans, you are *malum necessarium*."

The Nazis had courted Iceland before the war, extolling the qualities shared by all "Nordic" nations, instituting a chair of German at the University, and sending picked bands of young Nazis to work on farms and sell the new Germany to the Icelandic people.

Iceland was of vital strategic importance to the convoy routes between Britain and North America. As Churchill wrote, "It was upon this thought that, with the concurrence of its people, we had occupied Iceland when Denmark was overrun in 1940". Churchill had visited Iceland in August 1941 on his way back from meeting President Roosevelt at sea and signing the Atlantic charter, and had received rousing applause from the Icelanders as he stumped through Reykjavik waving his stick. He came in the battleship *Prince of Wales*, so soon and so dramatically to be sunk with the *Repulse* by the Japanese off Singapore.

CHAPTER 13

BOLT FROM THE BLUE

The days we spend in harbour give the Chief his chance for a renewed onslaught on the Captain's shower. Towards the evening of the third day Chief emerges, grimy and rust-bespattered but triumphant. All possible pipes have been taken adrift or blanked off, all joints and taps (there are at least six) have been stripped down. Both the hot and the cold water tanks are ready to perform. There is just one precaution.

"'S all right now," says Chief. "Only thing is that tap. Turn it to 'ot when you want it cold, like. 'Course I *could* put it on right way round ..."

We register expectation.

" ... Only then the *letterin'* would be upside down."

We call it a day.

The Captain hurried back on board. "The Admiral's coming down to inspect us at eleven this morning. Hands to be in working rig, and normal ship's routine to carry on. Just fall them in forrard. See we're not looking too awful."

I made a rapid round, revolving in my mind all the appalling things which could damn a ship for ever in an Admiral's eyes, from an untidy boat to an overlooked cleaning rag in the mess-deck. Some Admirals — and Captains — have an uncanny eye for the single solitary item which somehow got neglected in the general turmoil of preparation, whether an unpolished doorknob, a slack halliard or the funnel missing.

This inspection was brief and to the point. The Admiral came with only his Flag Lieutenant: he spoke to each man, asked him his Action Station, concentrating on the points most vital to our fighting efficiency. At the end he suggested some practical improvements. It was exactly right for a ship's company not so long away from fishing or civvy street, and inclined to believe "The Navy" more interested in "Pusser Routine" than getting the job done. They responded and were on their mettle. By the time we reached the after end of the ship the Captain and I were

85

congratulating ourselves on the good show, and breathing more freely at having got off without any conspicuous lapses. Then the Admiral, contrary to all expectation, suddenly dived through a door and down the ladder to the engine room. At the bottom he came face to face with the Third Engineman, Bill Bowie of Aberdeen. Bowie, having been on watch all the morning, had not heard that the Admiral was coming. The sight of so exalted a being in *Wastwater*'s engine room so astounded him that he stood gaping, incapable even of removing the cigarette which hung smouldering from his lower lip like a fish-hook, while the Captain and I groaned and gesticulated in vain.

"Take that thing out of your mouth," said the Admiral. He strode rapidly round the engine room, climbed up on deck and went forrard.

"A good ship and a good ship's company," he said to the Captain, as he stepped ashore and was gone.

The sequel to the Admiral's visit was not long delayed. The Captain was a little breathless when he got back from Operations. I was on deck, superintending the arrival of some stores. He spoke in a low voice. "I've got some bad news for you, old man: we're going to America. Come up to my cabin and I'll tell you about it."

"America! Very good, Sir; I'll just finish this, then I'll come up."

I forced myself to concentrate on getting the boxes properly stowed. My mind was in a turmoil, and there was a sick feeling at the pit of my stomach. Going to America! So this was the end of all our hopeful calculations about refit and the chances of my being at home when the baby came. To be together this time had been our hope and longing these last months. Now the sea would not have it. The malignant sea would come between us again. Last time I had at least been able to be at hand soon afterwards. Now ... a host of gruesome, unthinkable possibilities rose up and choked me. I hated the sea, the Admiralty, the war, the impersonal, senseless futility.

In the Captain's cabin, we talked it over, while he thoughtfully filled his pipe and drew once or twice to test the packing. He didn't know a great deal more: merely that we were being sent "for anti-submarine work off the North American continent". There were some trawlers going and two of us whalers from Iceland, ourselves and *Buttermere*. "The Admiral said he'd been told to send his two best ships," said the Captain. I made some unprintable comment. Still I was pleased. We both were. Gradually more cheerful possibilities began to appear on the horizon. Perhaps it would only be a brief sojourn; perhaps I might even yet be home in time; anything could happen.

But when I sat down to write to Honor, unable to tell her where we were bound, or for how long, or any of the important things, anger and desolation returned. We seemed to be looking into a yawning and limitless void. The news would be a heavy blow to hopes she had built so much on. And yet her phrase came back to me: we were a part of our generation. This was no more than so many of our generation had to bear. Many had it a lot worse. I knew that whatever happened to me, or to the baby even, she would never be left friendless or purposeless again. That certainty gave me heart and strength.

I began to think about the days ahead and to jot down a list of things to be seen to before we set off on our long ocean passage. It was a long list, ranging from "Change Icelandic money" to "Stores and water in sea-boats to be renewed". One item omitted might cost us dear. Our longest trip: in a way, an adventure. I began to kindle just a little with excitement. For the weed of self-pity, busy-ness can be a helpful weed-killer.

CHAPTER 14

TO RESCUE AMERICA

The North Atlantic during those March days of our passage showed itself mild and gentle as a lamb. We had a breeze astern and a huge following swell which came after us in a rise and fall like the sweep of English downs. Where big ships might have swung and pitched awkwardly, *Buttermere* and *Wastwater* rode easy and comfortable. It was a new experience for us. A mountain range of water, travelling perhaps twice our speed, would overtake us, but with so gentle an approach that it lifted us almost unaware. For a few moments we would be carried forward on the summit, while the beat of our propeller seemed to quicken with excitement, then it would pass on under our keel, and our bow would swing off a little as we sidled gently down the retreating slope into the next broad valley. It was only by watching *Buttermere* rise to full view and then sink till only her mast was visible that I realised how great was the dip between crest and trough.

"Close *Buttermere* a bit," said the Captain. "Don't forget we have to keep station on her."

Lieutenant G.F. Farrow, RNR (George to his friends), Commanding Officer of *Buttermere*, was our Senior Officer. Therefore to him had come the signal, "Being in all respects ready for war, take *Wastwater* under your command and proceed ..." etc. And, therefore, it was his privilege to regulate speed and course, while we kept station. Of course, that did not relieve us of responsibility for navigating our own ship. Nothing is easier than to get separated in bad weather and at night, with ships running totally darkened. And now the two of us were alone in the vast ocean, two tiny specks, pressing on by day and night, carrying our circle of visibility with us, like the spotlight that moves with a dancer. *Buttermere* looked minute; could we really be as small as that ourselves? We must stick together. Even so, we would be outgunned by a pack of U-boats should they choose to attack us, and we were off the route of any known shipping. Then there was always the chance of meeting a German raider, coming down, as the *Bismarck* had come a few months before, through the Denmark Strait, to sink the *Hood* before being sunk herself.

"Suppose we do meet one?" I asked. "We can't get within range, and we can't run away if we want to, we haven't the speed. What do we do then?"

The Captain wrinkled his brow over this delicate social problem. "Pretend not to notice," he decreed.

But the pale sun shone, and we saw neither ship nor aircraft; and many wonderful signs indicated what a smooth passage we were having. First, it was possible to open the lower half doors to the after flat. Invariably in Iceland this had meant the swamping of the after flat, followed by a cascade of water down the companion ladder into my cabin. Second, I was able to write some letters at my desk. This was a new phenomenon. I had often made the attempt before but after a few lines the paper began to get a spotty look and the ache behind my eyes somehow got linked up with a restless unease in my stomach, and I had to give it up. Turning the pages of picture magazines had proved the greatest mental exertion of which I was then capable. Now, however, I was able to write a daily bulletin while, above my head, the steering engine burst spasmodically into life, and below my feet the propeller shaft chattered steadily, and three thousand fathoms of water flowed between *Wastwater*'s keel and the ocean bed.

Another sign was a patch of white cement dust which had blown onto our gun platform from a tramp ship in Reykjavik harbour. Every morning as it got light I looked from the bridge to see whether wind or spray had carried that patch away, but it stayed there right across the Atlantic.

Every other day we put the clocks back, every morning as I watched the cook and steward emerge blinking from the hatch and make their way to the galley, the sun stood higher in the heavens. We were steering south as well as west.

Every forenoon the Captain, Jones and I would take our sextants onto the boat-deck and try our hand at "shooting the sun", while the Captain raked up his memories of navigation in the Merchant Service and began to initiate us into those mysterious rites. I had done plenty of coastal navigation, but this was different: deep-sea. For me it was the beginning of an intermittent enthusiasm which never left me, of a process I found fascinating for ever afterwards. To measure with a precise instrument the elevation of sun or star above the horizon, to take the exact time, to repeat the performance a second time, and then, by a series of calculations, to find the ship's latitude and longitude and plot the position on the chart: that gave me an endless satisfaction which was not the least diminished by my very hazy grasp of the reasons for what I was doing. I was no expert. If the doctor's prescription worked, that was good enough for me. A contemptible attitude, but reality. As I ploughed through unfamiliar tables and retraced my steps through faulty arithmetic, I appreciated for the first time the convention that two and two should make neither three nor five.

Each day we would gather in the Captain's cabin to reap the fruit of our labours. After a strenuous twenty minutes of pencil-plying and table-consulting, one of us would lead off :

"Well, what do you get?"

"Humm, I put us about ten miles north-west of the DR position."

"So do I — no, wait, I'm 30 miles south — ah, I see, I should have subtracted here where I've added, I think ... "

A pause.

"This looks more like it! No — oh blast, I've added in the date this time!"

But, as in golf, one successful stroke obliterates past failures. When, by some means or other, we made our landfall off the Newfoundland coast only eight miles from where we reckoned, after a voyage of 1,400 miles, the last twelve hours of it in fog, we felt an inner glow that was almost spiritual.

"Straight to New York," were the orders the Captain came back with at Halifax, adding: "It's fifteen years since I was in New York. You'll like New York." He called to Jones. "Make sure you get the latest information about entry into the harbour, Sub." It would be an anticlimax to run aground, or be sunk by a friendly coastal battery. Jones went ashore and came back with several new chart folios. We slipped that evening, and were off on the last lap.

There is a calm sea and a milder feeling in the air as we plough south-westerly for New York, *Buttermere* and ourselves. There is a subdued sense of excitement and an extra alertness. We know that there are a number of U-boats operating in the waters through which we are passing, and that ships have been sunk there recently, shelled and torpedoed.

In the morning, off Nantucket Shoals, there is fog about and visibility is down to a quarter of a mile. "Close to 1 cable," winks the lamp from *Buttermere*'s bridge, but even so it is difficult to keep station on her, a pale ghost retreating ever into the fog.

The Cox'n is on watch, and the Captain is on the bridge with him when one of the lookouts, newly joined before we left Iceland, remarks deferentially, "Periscope bearing green four-oh, Sir".

"Hard a-starboard! Where? Where?" shouts the Captain hoarsely, peering into the fog.

"Lost it now, Sir, it was just ..."

"Action stations!"

As the bells clang, Jones and the four-inch gun's crew project themselves like a swarm of bees onto the gun platform, the depth charges are got ready, and I dash for the bridge. As I arrive the Asdic operator is tensely searching for contact, and bodies are hanging out of all the bridge windows, peering into the fog.

"There he is, three hundred yards, red two-oh!"

"Fire!"

Bang! The bridge rocks, a column of water goes up off our port bow; I see a slim rod sticking up; the Lewis gunners see it and open fire with a deafening clatter. The next moment comes "Cease Fire". The "periscope" passes down our side, bobbing satirically, close enough for us to see, even in the fog, that it is the upper end of a dan-buoy stave, bored with a hole which looks for all the world like the business end of a periscope. "Well, Big Bertha made a nice bang anyway," says Jones, joining us on the bridge. "Personally I'd rather take no chances. That hole at the top now — I could have sworn I saw the monocled eye of a Prussian looking out."

Confirmation that we had found America came in an unexpected way. In Reykjavik, Jones, an ingenious fiddler, had put together a Heath-Robinson wireless set, sufficient to get the local Icelandic station, though not the BBC. It had died of natural causes, but as we approached New York, he strove to revive it. Suddenly, as we sat in the wardroom, through the impenetrable surrounding fog came a resonant American voice assuring us that Kellogg's breakfast food would double America's war effort. We were on course.

The Captain was excited at the thought of seeing New York again, and offered a packet of cigarettes to the first man to sight the Ambrose Lightship. But it was still foggy in my morning watch, and we came in along the south of Long Island, hugging the ten fathom line, navigating by soundings.

"We must be there by now," said the Captain anxiously, studying the chart, and at that moment we heard, somewhere ahead in the fog, the distant dreary moan of the lightship's fog signal, desolate as a cow lowing after her calf.

"Steer ten degrees to port."

Five minutes, ten minutes.

"There she is, sir," called half a dozen voices at once. We spelt out the name AMBROSE in huge letters on her side. Beyond all shadow of doubt we had arrived.

It is a moment we have waited for, and we are not disappointed. We are bringing HM Whaler *Wastwater*, our ship, up the Hudson River to New York. The pilot whom we have picked up hands us a morning paper, voluminous and headlined, but we do not read it yet. He points out the features on shore: Sandy Hook, Coney Island — "Sure, that's the parachute jump sticking up" — and presently the outskirts of Brooklyn and the forts. "There's Staten Island, that rising land to port; that's where you're to go now."

Jones is on the bridge with them, studying the chart for future reference. Alf is on the wheel: that broad form is steady as a rock; he might as well be steering us into Tokyo or Grimsby Dock. On deck Morrison and the hands are getting the wires and fenders ready for going alongside. Piratical sea-going garments are temporarily discarded, and they are all in clean rig for entering harbour. When everything is ready they fall in forrard and aft. Now, if ever, we must put on a good show.

As we move up harbour, the last shreds of fog melt away and the spring sun comes out, gleaming on the blue water, the crowded anchorage, the tugs and ferries plying busily, the piers and houses on Staten Island and, six miles across the water, the great skyscrapers on Manhattan, mounting up like petrified flames, like the turrets and pinnacles of a medieval castle. Even at this distance the impression of monumental size, of flamboyant grandeur, is overpowering. And in the foreground a small demure *Wastwater* moving confidently up harbour to her berth.

We have come here not as globe-trotting tourists, leaning on the rail of some floating hotel. We have come because we are needed. On the gun platform, Guns is giving a final polish to his glistening pet, the four-inch gun. Like everyone else he feels the drama of the moment. To the greatest, most spectacular city of the New World, unaware of our arrival, he announces reassuringly: "Courage, America. Help is on the way".

CHAPTER 15

WHY WE HAD TO COME

When Guns gave New York his assurance, "Courage, America, help is on the way", he spoke truer than any of us knew.

The battle of the Atlantic, Churchill's obsessive priority, began on the first day of the war and was not won until May 1945. But there were times in that period when it could have been lost. If the Atlantic life-line had been cut at any point, or so strangled that Britain was forced to make terms with Germany as Hitler hoped, there could have been no liberation of Europe.

In our minds, any idea of ultimate defeat and capitulation was unthinkable. And yet, that sunny Spring morning as we steamed up the Hudson, we were at a hinge of history.

Churchill wrote later that in the Atlantic the first six months of 1942 "proved the toughest of the whole war ... The U-Boat fleet ravaged American waters almost uncontrolled". He later confirmed that "The U-Boat attack was our worst evil. It would have been wise for the Germans to stake all upon it". General Marshall told US Admiral King, "The losses by submarines off our Atlantic seaboard and in the Caribbean now threaten our entire war effort".

For the U-Boats this was their "happy time". Admiral Doenitz wrote in his war diary on 17 January 1942, "*U-123* signals that they have achieved results far above expectations". Her Captain was Reinhold Hardegen, who brought his boat to the mouth of the Hudson, raised his periscope and told his crew that he could see the dancing girls on top of the Empire State Building. Virtually unopposed, the first five U-Boats of that Operation Drumbeat sank 25 ships in 2 weeks, most of them tankers; torpedoed a US destroyer off the Jersey coast; and ventured close inshore. Off Virginia Beach, Florida, a U-Boat in broad daylight sank a merchant ship by gunfire in sight of the holiday crowds.

Doenitz reported in dramatic terms: "Our U-boats are operating close inshore along the coast of the United States of America, so that bathers and sometimes entire coastal cities are witnesses to the drama of war, whose visual climaxes are constituted by the red glorioles of blazing tankers".

Continued losses on this scale would be catastrophic for beleaguered Britain, where fuel needs amounted to four large tankers a day. British urgings for a convoy system had been resisted by the American Admiral Ernest J. King, who preferred a "patrol and search" policy.

Neither by sea nor by air was America prepared for the needs of coastal convoy. A desperate Churchill later wrote, "On 10 February, we offered unasked 24 of our best-equipped anti-submarine trawlers and 11 corvettes with their trained crews to the US Navy". That was how *Buttermere* and *Wastwater* came to spend the next eight months based at New York, defending America's east coast. King was obliged to accede, but it was not until June that he publicly acknowledged that escorted convoys were the only effective defence against U-boats.

In the midst of events, we were unaware of these top-level strategic debates governing our destinies. But the American historian Michael Gannon has made a recent review and summing-up in his book, *Operation Drumbeat* (1990). He assesses the U-boat campaign on America's east coast as far more serious than Japan's dramatic attack on Pearl Harbour, which focused the anger and outrage of most Americans, but which left intact the all-important aircraft carriers. In US Navy-protected waters on the east coast, an aggregate of 397 ships were sunk in the first half of 1942, with a loss of perhaps 5,000 men of the navy and merchant marine, for negligible losses of U-boats. Gannon rates it "one of the greatest maritime disasters in history, and the American nation's worst-ever defeat at sea". He concludes that "What really broke the back of the U-boat campaign in US waters was the coastal convoy".

This was made possible by the multiplication of small craft with anti-submarine equipment. There were 31 sinkings by U-boats in January, mostly tankers, and 69 in February. Our group of what the American press described as "rusty British trawlers" arrived in March. By the beginning of April, US Admiral Andrews was able to institute his "Bucket Brigade" of daylight convoys, with British anti-submarine escorts. Sinkings declined dramatically, though few U-boats were sunk. Eventually, in mid-July, Doenitz withdrew his U-boats elsewhere, to the Caribbean and mid-Atlantic. The American coastline was no longer "happy" for them.

While operating from New York we ourselves never sighted a U-boat on the surface. But their handiwork was visible enough: masts and wrecks in shallow water close inshore. Before the convoys were started we carried out a night patrol southward. Presently we met a sight which startled and alarmed us with its novelty: a large merchant ship northbound, with all her lights blazing, evidently relying on her neutrality as a safeguard. Later we learned that she had been torpedoed and sunk soon after we passed her.

Coastal shore lights north and south of Atlantic City had only recently been extinguished, as for three months proprietors protested at the damage such restrictions would do to their tourist businesses. Pearl Harbour had focused American passions and the bulk of their naval forces on the war in the Pacific, but it took time for Americans to grasp the reality of the threat on their Atlantic doorstep.

CHAPTER 16

SAILORS IN WONDERLAND

The tense controversies over convoy policy which had preceded our coming had no effect on our reception at the working level, which could not have been more cordial. I went with the Captain on his first visit to 90 Church Street, the US Navy Headquarters in New York, when Commander Pierce, our operational chief, gave us a businesslike outline of the job planned for us, listened closely to our suggestions, accepted an invitation to visit, and was a genial and entertaining lunch guest. Later we had a day of General Drills, when a group of USN officers inspected the ship and came to sea with us while we fired our guns, dropped depth charges, sent away boats, exercised Fire, Collision and every other sort of drill. Their official report was thorough, including some recommendations for improvement.

One comment showed a generosity not always evident in inter-service assessments. Of our Asdic ratings they reported: "Operators well-trained and efficient — much better than ours".

Sometimes admiration could be almost embarrassing. Ship-handling was something that interested me, and the Captain often left it to me. One day I had turned out of the Hudson and brought *Wastwater* alongside our berth at Pier Fourteen. Mooring lines, springs and fenders were secured. I called down "Finished with engines", and came down from the bridge. A USN Lieutenant on the quay approached me.

"I was watching you come in. That was a fine bit of sea-manship."

My performance, which was fairly much routine, could hardly vie with that of the Captain of the *Queen Mary* who, during a tug strike, docked his ship in New York without tugs. All the same, who objects to a word of spontaneous commendation? Equally spontaneous was the reaction of the US Coastguard sailor who looked down from the quay to our deck and asked incredulously, "Did you guys really cross the Atlantic in that thing?"

From the start our stay in New York was no sinecure. After

a few preliminary patrols we settled down to the regular job of escorting convoys between the Hudson and the Delaware. Between 4 and 5 am we would slip from the silent piers and feel our way down harbour, through the dark anchorage, past buoys flashing red, white or green, down the long channel to the sea, where our convoy of merchant ships would be forming up at first light. Immediately we would be hailed by a swarm of small US boats and launches, known generally as Yippies. We were the Senior Officer Escorts, the Big Ship, as we stationed our group of Yippies according to their number, equipment, etc., like a Fleet Admiral deploying his destroyer flotillas and cruiser squadrons.

Besides keeping an eye on the escorts, we had to watch the merchant ships, spurring on the laggards and restraining individualists who streamed away regardless of the convoy speed, and who at first understood neither flag signals nor our Loud Hailer.

A cheerful voice from the bridge of a palpitating tramp steamer, to whom we have closed to shout, "Slow Down!": "Sorry, old boy, don't speak your lingo — I'm a Greek!"

We had a procession of blue sunny days and calm seas, while the flat sandy coastline crept by, broken only by rows of houses, clearly visible, the high water-towers typical of that coast, and the tall buildings of Atlantic City. We navigated by buoys and wrecks, some of them showing the tops of masts, others with whole bows still above water. Reaching the Delaware about dusk, we would supervise the entry of the convoy, then anchor ourselves, or patrol, picking up the northbound convoy at dawn the next morning.

Buttermere and ourselves were so employed for five months, spending four or five days at sea, with sometimes little more than 24 hours in harbour for storing, getting any defects repaired, visiting 90 Church Street and seeing New York. It was a busy routine. All the same, we were the envy of colleagues in the other trawlers, as the two ships lucky enough to be based on New York.

The transformation in our lifestyle was unbelievable. Apart from the Captain and Morrison, who had been there before, New York was for most of us an unfolding marvel. For me it was also a discovery of America.

Pier Fourteen, our base, was a striking demonstration of the American faculty for speedy provision and getting things done. When we arrived, it was little more than a bare wooden jetty. Long before we left, it comprised, with the adjacent pier, a fully equipped base with operational offices, victualling stores from which we drew all our provisions, naval stores with all our normal requirements (cleaning materials, paint, rope, etc.) electrical and technical offices, and workshops which could deal with all but major engineering defects. More than that, it boasted a "diner" of its own, recreation rooms for the US enlisted men and our ratings, and (a great boon to us all), hot shower baths, which really worked.

During our whole stay in New York the Chief suspended all his operations on the Captain's shower. Finally, with the warm weather, there arrived on the Pier a glistening machine which, for a nickel, would produce from its vitals a paper cup and fill it, according to your choice at the press of a button, with Coca-cola, lemon and lime, or root beer. (Now commonplace world-wide, these wonders were a revelation to us.)

Being victualled by the US Navy, we shared their more elaborate menus, and such delicacies as chicken, ice cream, fruit juices and breakfast foods became part of our bill of fare. In the wardroom we favoured cold salad lunches and were grateful for the liberal supplies of eggs, ham, lettuce and other vegetables. Messdeck taste however remained more conservative. Even in the hottest summer weather no fancy dishes supplanted the prime and original favourites: roast with two veg, gravy and liberal lumps of duff as a first course; and for pudding a real, good, solid duff, with raisins or jam sauce. Duff was the thing: and if it came up on the heavy side, with a wet, shiny look like liver when you cut it: well, there'd be no complaints from the messdeck on *that* score.

New York in the spring of 1942 had barely felt the touch of wartime restrictions. We gazed incredulously at shop windows crammed with chocolates, fruit and sumptuous uncouponed materials; at US sailors throwing away half-smoked "see-gars"; at restaurant menus as long as your arm; and Sunday newspapers of thirty or forty pages, including supplements, to provide a family with reading matter for a week. And it was all laid on so conveniently, so temptingly. Inside the Staten Island ferry terminus was all one could want in the normal span of life: bookstalls, "sodas", telephones, telegraph and cable office, hairdresser, confectioner, florist and a "diner" where, perched on a stool, you could have anything from doughnuts and coffee through to hamburgers or an ample three-course meal.

The British Navy was still something of a novelty. Our uniforms were unfamiliar and indeed uniforms of any kind still had glamour to a populace only just getting used to the idea of being at war. Some greetings were unusual. Several beards had been grown during our stay in Iceland but none so fine as Alf Holtby's: black, bushy and circular in shape, giving him rather the expression of a benevolent Father Christmas. The beard, however, was unknown in the US Navy and Alf became "the Bearded Sailor" and a man of note. One day as he strolled with some shipmates along Broadway, a bevy of admiring girls surrounded him. One of them, taking a firm hold of his beard, gave it a tug, exclaiming, "Look girls — it's *real!*"

Our sailors could go ashore for the evening without a cent in their pockets. Sure enough before they had walked a mile, a car would pull up and a head would lean out: "Say, where are you boys from in the old country? I got a cousin in Liverpool, England, myself. Jump in and come along home".

Or else it would be an emigrant from Britain who had settled in the USA but was delighted to hear the news and speech of the old country. Several of our crew made friends with such families in Staten Island and went regularly to their homes in their "watch ashore". Others, notably the Scots, chose their society strictly on national lines. Morrison and Cameron discovered a Caledonian Society where the former achieved such distinction as a sword dancer that he was televised throughout New York. Another Scot, John McIver, was different. He made one trip "across the water" to Manhattan soon after we arrived and never went there again. McSweeney's Bar, just outside the Pier Gate, was far enough.

When I remarked on this he merely smiled. "Ah, one place is much like another, so I didn't go again. I thought, well, I'll just not bother."

For most, however, New York was dazzling and inviting. We suddenly had the problem — almost unknown in Iceland — of men overstaying shore leave.

"Seaman Palfry, absent over leave two hours, thirty minutes, namely from 0700 to 0930," recited the Coxswain.

"But you say, Palfry, that you boarded the ferry at 0100?" The Captain was puzzled.

"Yes, Sir."

"But it didn't take you eight hours to travel from Battery Point to Staten Island!"

"Oh, no, Sir: but every time I woke up again, I was back at Battery Point, Sir."

The Stage Door Canteen (newly opened), Jack Dempsey's Bar, Coney Island, the stage and screen shows of Broadway and Times Square: we heard tales of them all, and many other wonders of New York, during quiet afternoon watches at sea, when a certain amount of talking on the bridge might be permissible. Bunts, a Londoner, usually to be relied on for a critical whinge of some kind, was lyrical, revealing a fastidious streak. "A lovely meal it was, Sir — clean plates, clean knives, clean cups, everything clean. And then clean little paper serviettes — just a little thing, but it made all the difference."

Lancashire Louis, Asdic operator, reported enthusiastically on Johnny Weissmuller in films of Tarzan. "You see 'im swinging about from tree to tree — 'e's proper useful lad in t' joongle, is Tarzan!"

However, Louis also disclosed some national characteristics and contrasts. "Trooble with Yanks," he told us, "when they've bought y' a drink, they have to tell ya that everything in America is best in t' world!"

"So, do you tell 'em what Britain does best?"

"Naw — why should I — when everyone knows?"

George Smillie was ready for anything. The Captain, sponsoring the cause of literature and art, arranged for a visit to a New York gallery exhibiting examples of modern Surrealist art. He took Alf, the indefatigable Bunts, and George, who was asked by the Gallery's Director what he thought of one of the exhibits. "Well," said George, without hesitation, "I reckon the feller who did that had a good load on board."

George was also prime mover in what proved one of our happiest parties on board, when the children from a nearby Convent School visited the ship, escorted by two competent and appreciative teaching Sisters who compared our housekeeping methods with those of their convent, while the small boys roamed the ship under the watchful eyes of Guns and of George, who later escorted the party back to the convent and stayed to take a glass of lime juice with the Mother Superior.

George was also the master-diplomat (I heard this later) in saving Roddy Campbell from himself. Roddy was the gentlest, most amenable of men, except after a certain intake of alcohol, when he became immensely stubborn. Returning to the ship just before leave expired, he sat down on a bollard and refused to go aboard. His friends pleaded, "Come on Roddy," all in vain.

"I'm not going back aboard that bastard!"

A plot was devised. George went a little way off on the quay and began to roll about drunkenly. His friends came to Roddy. "Roddy, we're having a bit of trouble with George. He's had a few too many and we can't get him back on board. Will you give us a hand?"

Such an appeal was irresistible. "Oho, drunk is he? Aye, I'll help. Come along now, George, come along. You're all right, man." And so, the drunk man assisting the sober, the little party returned on board and made their way without incident to the messdeck.

New York conditions made it possible to lift our level of cleanliness and housekeeping several notches. I made a rule that all flats, decks and messes had to be scrubbed out daily. This was resisted at first but later accepted. I made a daily round of all living spaces at eleven each morning as a counter to the dirt and disorder which threatened our crowded and varied company. When some of our ex-fishermen, usually the chief protesters at this fussiness, returned from a visit to another trawler with caustic comments about their "filthy bloody messdecks", I felt the struggle was not in vain. In this matter, the general smartness of the American small craft around us was a help. I commented on this whenever possible in the hearing of our crew, and also learned some practical improvements from our American friends.

We had return visits with the CO of a US Navy tug at Pier Fourteen. One day he brought a USN Lieutenant over for a drink. After some general comparing of notes, the visitor offered the comment, as a revealed truth, that in the British Navy the difference between officers and men was much wider than in the US Navy. To our friend he said, "That's so, isn't it, Jim?" Said Jim: "You could be surprised".

However, King's Regulations and Admiralty Instructions (KR & AI) ruled us, in New York as elsewhere. "Who's that new man?" the Captain asked, seeing the additional signalman who had just been sent to us. "He looks like an actor." In fact he was an actor and had belonged to a well-known repertory company. It caused much amusement in the messdeck when it was discovered that the New Bunts' idea of recreation was to sit reading in his mess in green shirt and green corduroy trousers. He weathered all comments, patiently submitted to being called "Dearie" by Old Bunts, and developed quite an impassioned fervour for scrubbing down the bridge. Soon after joining he was arraigned before the Captain for overstaying his leave. When asked the reason, he produced his most engaging smile and began, "Well, *actually,* it's rather a long story ...". The Captain's exclamation, as he awarded the statutory penalty, was something between a bellow, a snort and a common explosion. Thereafter New Bunts' stories became shorter. He became an accepted asset to our company.

We also received a steward who actually was a steward, with peace-time experience in Orient Line passenger ships. He added a touch of class to the three-step journey between galley and wardroom. Later, in Atlantic hurricanes, he fully proved his professionalism.

Then, while my thoughts kept turning to Britain and Honor, and the new life we expected, death came unexpectedly among us.

Stoker Pendleton was one of the quietest and best-liked men in the ship. He had the gentleness often found in those who have suffered long ill-health. From time to time he would come to me to have boils dressed: he told me that a number of doctors had examined him without discovering the origin or remedy of his complaint. Each time he came it was with an apologetic reluctance to cause any trouble with his unimportant affliction. He never looked well, but protested always that he felt all right, and took more than his full share of work, in mess deck and stokehold. His condition never seemed to change much for better or for worse. Therefore it came as a complete surprise to me when Chief said one day at sea, "You'd better 'ave a look at Pendleton; looks about all-in to me".

With a temperature of 104 he was induced, only under sternest orders, to leave the stokehold and turn into his bunk. We signalled for a hospital launch, and made full speed for the harbour entrance. In hospital a few hours later his temperature was normal, but he was retained for observation. By evening it was 105. After two weeks of tenuous existence, with many and conflicting symptoms of physical derangement which defied the best diagnosis, he died. He was buried close by the naval hospital, in a cemetery in Brooklyn, Long Island.

We were under sailing orders on the afternoon of the funeral; but our Colours were half-masted, I mustered all hands on the narrow boat-deck, and we all stood bare-headed while the Captain read a short prayer from the Burial Service, so wise and full of comfort, so devoid of all tragedy or despair. The caps were replaced, the Colours run up again, and the work of the ship went on.

The Chief, resourceful and helpful, arranged for the sale of Pendleton's belongings among his shipmates, and for sending the money, together with a photograph of the grave, to his only relative, his mother. To me fell the task of writing to tell her all

I could of the circumstances of her boy's death; to let her know that he had had the fullest and best attention to the end; that he had been a good shipmate; and had done his duty in the best cause (as I believed) that any man had ever lived or died for.

Her reply came weeks afterwards. Ted, as I knew, was her only son; he had always been a good son. She thanked us sincerely for thinking of her, but her circumstances would be sufficient. Ted had been happy in the ship; she was grateful, and wished us all good luck. It was not what she said, but the way she said it, that was moving in its dignity, the letter of one who, broken in heart, was unbroken in spirit. So we lost Ted Pendleton, a good stoker, a good shipmate, and a gentleman.

The twenty minute ferry ride from Staten Island to Battery Point, the southern tip of Manhattan — "the best five cents' worth in New York" — was our spectacular gateway to the Big Apple. There was the size and variety of the harbour, with merchant ships and warships at anchor, the continuous traffic of self-important tugs, train-ferries, floating cranes, the occasional liner and numerous small launches. Beyond towered the mountain range of sky-scrapers. I had seen photographs, but was unprepared for the breathtaking beauty, particularly towards evening, when the faint tints of green and orange and pale pink seemed to glow in the loftier buildings, studded with lights in their myriad windows.

By day the ferries were crowded. There were the boot-blacks, with their insidious "Sh-sh," "sh-sh," eyeing suggestively the shoes of likely customers; the throngs of boys and girls on holiday, often attired in the exotic uniform of some young peoples' band (there seemed few days without a parade of some kind); the girls and women, who, endowed with no greater natural beauty than their sisters in Britain, were able, with no war-time restrictions, to achieve a much higher level of charm and variety in their choice of clothes and hats.

Those journeys stirred Jones' wayward muse to produce an inspired poem, in the Lancashire style of Stanley Holloway. It told how a ferry-boat captain, frustrated by his restricted scope, took his ferry out to sea and sank a U-boat. The climax came with the lines,

> He hadn't no depth bombs, but he'd plenty of pluck;
> So he opened the gates and dropped a 20-ton truck.

The U-boat crew were taken prisoner; but in the excitement of his success, the Captain forgot the way home. However the vessel was put on the right course by one of the boot-blacks, who had been a proficient Boy Scout,

> But 'twas in navigation he'd come out best
> By remembering sun always set in west.

All ended happily with a reception by Mayor La Guardia in Times Square. The poem, with illustrations, was published in *Newsweek* of 21 October 1942.

Tale of the Ferryboat That Met a U-Boat

> I'll tell you a tale of a Ferryboat Captain
> Whose longest trip was Manhattan to Staten.
>
> And this occupation I think you'll agree,
> Ain't exciting enough if you're born to the sea.
>
> Now he craved for adventure 'cause his life was so dull,
> And he worried so much he was losing his wool.
>
> So one starlit night 'e could stand it no longer;
> He cried — "'ard-a-port, George, let's see what's out yonder."
>
> Now George 'e were 'elmsman, and held a clean ticket,
> And breaking firm's rules; well, it weren't playing cricket.
>
> But he stood to his post; like Centurion of old,
> Till his rose-budding nose turned blue with the cold.

And Captain he smiled as he paced on the bridge,
Though the wind, through the swing doors made saloon like a
    fridge.

Now most of the passengers were beginning to worry;
They wanted to go home and were in rather a hurry.

But Captain was deaf, to their pleas and their cries;
And quoted some poetry, about seas and the skies.

And not to be outdone friend George beat the band,
With one about Nelson and old Pen-in-t'hand.

So the passengers soon settled down to their plight,
And made preparations for stopping the night.

They moved all drunks and rolled them on the floor,
To help stop the wind blowing in under door.

Next morning, the sea had got a bit high,
And a nasty big cloud covered half of the sky.

But Captain stood there like a man in a dream,
Till George gave him a shove saying, "What's that on the
    beam?"

It were dirty big U-boat out on the prowl,
Complete with Commander, eye-glass and scowl.

But Captain kept cool, he'd been in worse spots,
And he bawled down the voice pipe for a dozen more knots.

Now the Chiefie he swore, 'cause his engines were knocking
And the language he used — was really quite shocking.

He was having some trouble with Big End and Straps,
And one of his stop valves was whistling Taps.

In meantime U-boat had been proper busy,
Firing torpedoes until he was dizzy.

But George he excelled in the art of his calling,
And evaded tin fish in a manner appalling.

So the U-boat submerged to escape a collision.
It were, you'll agree, a wise sort of decision.

But Captain continued; he'd got an idea,
And swore if successful, he'd buy George a beer.

He hadn't no depth bombs, but he'd plenty of pluck;
So he opened the gates and dropped a 20-ton truck.

'Twas a good way of dealing with old Mr. Hun,
And provided all hands with plenty of fun.

So they forgot all their troubles, and raised a wild cheer.
And they all started talking of prize money and beer.

The Nazis were captured and taken on board,
And Commander gave Captain his gilt-hilted sword.

It were all very fancy, but really no use,
The blade was all chipped, and the handle was loose.

The Captain was pleased, and said — "Thanks very much, sir,
If I'm sure you don't mind I'll give it our butcher.

Happen he'll mend it, and sharpen the blade,
Then wave it at folks when their bills are unpaid."

Then the Captain decided the best thing to do,
Was to set sail for home and George thought so too.

But when ship was turned round, the Captain said — "Hey!
Believe me or not, George, I've forgotten the way."

But as fate would have it, their good luck held out;
One of the Bootblacks had been a Boy Scout.

He learned knots and splices, and plenty of tricks;
Such as lighting a fire by rubbing two sticks.

But 'twas in navigation he'd come out best,
By remembering Sun always set in West.

So they followed the Sun, for more than an hour —
Till someone on top sighted Parachute Tower.

And all the passengers ran to the side,
They all felt so happy that some of them cried.

An hour or so later they were safely on land,
A bit disappointed there wasn't a band.

But Ferry Inspector was waiting on stage.
He was looking for Captain and weren't half in a rage.

Crying — "Where have you been for the last day or so?"
And Captain, being truthful, said, "I really don't know.

But we've sunk old U-boat, and captured some Huns;
And invented a depth charge, that weighs 20 tons."

So a policeman was sent for, and they told him their tale,
The Huns were arrested and locked up in jail.

At last news of the exploit reached the ears of the Mayor,
Who arranged a reception to be held in Times Square.

And Captain was granted a lifelong desire,
To ride with the Mayor to the next City Fire.

The Bootblack got Boy Scout's Wayfarer's Star,
And George a half share in Jack Dempsey's Bar.

Then the Chiefie got medal for his daring and pluck,
And U-boat Commander — got the bill for the truck.

The ferry rides introduced us to the insatiable curiosity of the American public. A perfect stranger would approach: "Excuse me, but what is that gold insignia on your arm? British Navy? Is that so?" And the conversation might pass to our opinion on the weather, baseball, or the Allied grand strategy.

An obviously new "enlisted man" at the ferry station dug me in the ribs, and indicating an officer wearing the three gold bands and gold-edged cap peak of a US Navy Commander, enquired, "Say, he's one o' the high-ups, ain't he?" The enquiry was not disrespectful, merely comradely.

Questions were frank, sometimes indignant. "You're British? Say, why don't the British give India freedom?" I began to discuss it; but he wanted an immediate answer. Defensively I said, "Maybe we should. But how is your race problem in America?" He froze. "We have no race problem. There is *no* race problem in America." He walked off.

While the battle for North Africa wavered to and fro, and Rommel's attack threatened Egypt and a junction with Germany's Japanese allies, we were asked, "When are the British going to quit running?" From others we met overwhelming admiration for Britain's gallantry under the blitz, conveyed by media coverage and Greer Garson in the film *Mrs Miniver*.

What New York offered in that first acquaintance, in contrast to London, where so many hidden treasures had to be discovered by research, was the gift of inspired showmanship, along with endless variety. Travelling north from Battery Point you would find a traditional church buried among the skyscrapers, or a square like a London square, quiet, genteel, with rails and gardens. After Greenwich Village we would find ourselves at Radio City and the Rockefeller Centre, perhaps the best expression of the invincible and extravagant optimism which characterised New York before the great financial crash. Even the sunken open-air skating rink, a human focus, seemed to cater only for two extremes: the elegant experts describing flawless figures on the ice, and the inevitable sailors falling over each other and providing a much appreciated comic relief. There was Times Square with its theatres, movies, scintillating lights, its cigarette advertisement emitting periodic puffs of smoke the size of a small thundercloud; Central Park; Broadway; and Grand Central Station, an underground marvel, free of grime and noise, proving that it was possible for a metropolitan terminus to be clean, quiet, dignified and convenient. Occasional forays north to the Bronx or east to Brooklyn unveiled the backstage drabness of life for so many of New York's millions.

For me personally our stay in New York was transformed by two heartening developments. The first was the publication of my book *The Jervis Bay and Other Poems*. The Captain's experience in publishing and the book trade, as well as his acquaintance with America, was a key to this happy event after the failure of Honor's efforts with publishers in Britain.

The US edition was published by the old-established firm of G.P. Putnam's Sons, who arranged also for publication in England by their London branch. Four thousand copies of the collection, which included my Newdigate Prize poem *Milton Blind* were sold in the USA, Britain, Australia and elsewhere. Putnams' director, Earle Balch, presided over the arrangements with gracious old-world courtesy, and invited Jones and me to stay with him overnight in his charming modest house in Reading, Connecticut. He explained that the almost universal use of timber rather than stone for houses in the district was due to the accident that carpenters predominated over masons in the first shipload of settlers.

The publication of Jones' ferry-boat poem in *Newsweek* was a literary double for *Wastwater*. I took the poem to Gracie Fields, who was then performing in New York, and made my way to her room in the Waldorf-Astoria (my uniform no doubt assisting my reception). While her husband, Montie Banks, blew champagne over a bowl of flowers to revive their bloom, she took the poem, which I hoped she might include in her programme; but alas, she thought the New York listeners would not understand it.

111

The second stroke of good fortune was the presence in New York of Archie Mackenzie, whom I had met in Oxford before the war through Oxford Group friends. Archie, an able and knowledgeable Scot, after taking his degree had won a Commonwealth Scholarship to study in America, and was now working in the British Press Service. He guided my inexperienced steps in a press interview about my book; and more importantly, introduced me to an American family, Han and Virginia Twitchell and their three children. Their hospitable home in East 71st Street was a haven throughout my stay, where I knew I was welcome whenever I could get an evening ashore. There I met from time to time Ted (Admiral Sir Edward) Cochrane, also a Scot, who had been called back from retirement to be Commodore of convoys to and fro across the Atlantic, in which service he was kind enough to take letters and small gifts for Honor. In his responsible role as Commodore, Ted won the gratitude of the masters of his merchant ships, who usually found signalling a burden, by reducing his instructions to an absolute minimum. He made many Atlantic crossings without being sunk.

The Twitchells invited me to their family's delightful holiday house on Long Island and also arranged for me to pay a visit, by overnight Pullman car and at their expense, to Detroit, for a unique occasion. This was the premiere performance of *The Forgotten Factor*, a play written by my Oxford friend Alan Thornhill, formerly Chaplain of Hertford College, who had come to work full-time with Dr Frank N.D. Buchman, the American of Swiss-German descent, who was the founder of Moral Re-Armament and who was then in America.

The international group accompanying him were concentrating their utmost efforts on the task of strengthening America's morale and mobilising her huge resources for the vital business of war production. They had already toured in twenty states with a revue, *You Can Defend America*. Thornhill's new play embodied similar ideas in a story of clash and reconciliation between a passionate trade-union strike leader and a stubborn industrial manager, with their families on both sides involved. I was immediately captured by the convincing reality of the characters and incidents, which held the audience spellbound. Here was a compelling play, a human drama in its own right, which conveyed its message without a breath of preaching. The theme was simple but profound: that the most stubborn conflicts can be resolved when individuals change, acknowledge the forgotten factor that God has a plan and a solution, and seek common ground on the basis of what is right, rather than who is right.

The Detroit premiere was in the Ford Theatrette, and our hostess was Mrs Henry Ford, who was a friend of Buchman. The author Alan Thornhill, English of the English, had achieved a trans-national tour de force.

An incredulous lady in the audience exclaimed, "I can't believe that play was written by an Englishman. It's *American!*"

Alan's rapport with America was not confined to the writing of plays. He later married a refreshingly uninhibited American girl, Barbara van Dyke.

The play, though American in its original setting, proved to have a universal human impact. Presented round the world in the following years, it sparked responses from audiences not only in the USA, Britain, Australia and New Zealand, but in Asian countries including India, Pakistan and Ceylon. Its message of change and reconciliation remained as relevant to post-war reconstruction as the immediate task of winning the war. But it was in the immediate war-time context that Senator Truman, Chairman of the Senate Committee investigating war contracts, recognised its value. In April 1944, after seeing the play, he told a Washington Press Conference.

Suspicions, rivalries, apathy, greed lie behind most of the bottlenecks ... The Moral Re-Armament group have rolled up their sleeves and gone to work. They have already achieved remarkable results in bringing teamwork into industry ... If America does not catch this spirit we shall be lucky to win the war and certain to lose the peace. With it there is no limit to what we can do for America, and America for the world.

113

A year later, with Roosevelt's death, Truman was President.

In Detroit I met Frank Buchman briefly for the first time. Aged sixty-six, he was still exhausted and frail from a serious heart attack which had almost cost him his life. No one could have foreseen that his most important and influential work still lay ahead. At an evening party, as we sat together, he turned to me and asked one question: did I find the practice of the "quiet time", the regular habit of seeking direction from a wisdom greater than one's own, was helpful in my day-to-day life?

The story of my discovery of America would be incomplete without the story of Yolande, which was also a story of discovering things about myself. Buchman's totally dispassionate question to me in the few minutes of our conversation became lodged in my mind and played its part. So did the words of the Greek philosopher Socrates, four hundred years before Christ. For Socrates, the base and foundation of wisdom was "Know yourself". I thought I did: but I had some way to go, and needed help.

Yolande was an attractive French-Canadian girl whom Jones and I met at an afternoon reception arranged for British service visitors by society ladies of New York. We introduced ourselves, chatted a while, and as we left, she invited us to a concert. She evidently enjoyed life, and had a sense of humour, salted with a dry Gallic scepticism which appealed to me. She came from a convent school in Canada, but had moved to New York with her family and now had a secretarial job. Presently she and I began to meet regularly for lunch, supper, or a film. To be seen in company with a British naval uniform was no disadvantage in New York at that time; but we genuinely enjoyed each other's company in a relaxed style. She was deeply impressed by Greer Garson as the heroic British housewife in the film *Mrs Miniver*.

She shared an apartment with her mother and brother and took me to meet them. I had told her that I was married and talked about Honor and the baby we were expecting. Yolande's style was casual and light-hearted. When she detected that her animated conversational mother was trying to impress me, she interjected, "Lay off, Mother; I saw him first".

114

Her parents were living apart but were on amicable terms, and her father called in to meet me. After some general talk, he asked, "You're married, aren't you? How would your wife feel about this?" What I mumbled in reply is not clear in my mind. I remember a sense of discomfort, and a disinclination to pursue the subject. I argued that my relationship with Yolande was a pleasant and companionable friendship, which we both enjoyed. She made no attempts to draw me in the direction of sexual intimacy. I don't think we even kissed. Kissing then was considered more emotionally significant than today's casual, indiscriminate or off-hand procedures. I believed I had the situation well in control. Anyway I enjoyed it.

Two more incidents intervened to disturb my comfort and counteract the sedation of my conscience. In a haphazard general discussion in the wardroom about New York's attractions and the shore-going diversions of our ship's company, a voice — whose I don't know — said, amidst laughter, "Anyway, the married men are the worst". I brushed the incident and the thought away. But it kept coming back. In a company as small and close as *Wastwater*'s not much was missed, not much went unobserved.

The final incident was conclusive. My regular visits to the Twitchells' home were an unqualified boon, as well as a precious link with England and Honor. Although she never said so, she probably felt it also as a valued anchor and security for me in my physical, mental or emotional world-wanderings.

One evening the Twitchells invited me to dinner with Archie Mackenzie. It was a relaxed, congenial occasion, but as the meal concluded I rose to leave. Surprised, they protested that it was still early; did I have to go? I explained that I had duties which called me back to the ship. But in fact I had arranged to meet Yolande. We had supper together at a restaurant before I caught a late ferry back to Staten Island and *Wastwater*. But I had now to face something clear and unequivocal. I had told a deliberate lie to people who believed in me and trusted me. Scales fell from my eyes as I confronted an ugly reality about my nature, beginning with self-deception. My feelings for Yolande were leading me in

115

the wrong direction. Why else would I conceal the truth from my friends? I saw the forked roads, the beginning of a double life. I had learned something about the serpentine process which begins with a lie in the soul. It was a turning point. I told Honor, who was forgiving.

I saw Yolande once or twice before we left New York. We remained friends but everything was different. She wrote; and later told me she was marrying Harry, a British Merchant Navy Officer.

It was years afterwards that I told the full story to Archie, asking forgiveness for my dishonesty. He had no recollection or blame. But a canker in my own conscience was revealed and healed.

Regular mail was one of New York's greatest boons to us. Any news is better than none. Not much of it was good during those months. In the Pacific the Allies were fighting a grim rearguard action to stave off the threatened Japanese advance on Hawaii and Australia, where McArthur had just set up his headquarters. "McArthur Buttons" were being sold all over New York; Australia was much in the news. My father's letters brought news of American uniforms in the streets of Ballarat, our home town. He shared the general view that the Americans' arrival (with virtually the bulk of Australian forces and all the equipment still in the Middle East), had narrowly saved Australia from invasion. In Africa the British armies were struggling desperately to avert the catastrophe of an Axis advance to the Nile and the Suez Canal: the U-boat campaign was still taking heavy toll in the Atlantic; the RAF had launched their great offensive in Europe, but sharp German raids on Britain continued.

Chief heard that his wife and the kids had been blitzed: no injuries, but the younger boy suffering from shock. They had gone back to Hull from the country for a few days' holiday. "Told 'er to keep away an' all. I'd teach 'er, if I was there." Chief spoke with the sudden fierceness of a frightened man.

To one of our Grimmies came word that his brother had been lost at sea in a cruiser. Rationing, the blackout, the call-up of

116

younger women, these were no more than the price to be expected by a nation totally mobilised in war. But they brought us back from the great, milling, preoccupied world of New York to the cold reality that our way of life was being guarded by the blood, toil, tears and sweat, of men and women. There seemed a touch of unreality about newspaper reports and news flashes which gave the impression that warfare consisted entirely of "blasting hell out of Japs".

In Honor's letters, forwarded after some delay, one thought kept recurring, the chances of my return.

22 Feb. Now at last I have some idea where you are. I realised just how much I had been counting on your coming home in time. The lower lip trembled a bit I'm afraid; but later I felt quite sure that these fresh circumstances need make no difference.

How lovely if you could be back for Easter! It's nearly four months now since you went; and we did think six possible ...

I'm sending on a hamper of food from Sandy in Australia, it's addressed to you.

I'm getting everything of the best here, truly, and feeling very well ...

17 May. Had quite a comfortable journey across to York. The blitz has been bad there, but fortunately they missed the Minster and wall. It was looking lovely as a dream with all the spring foliage and soft clouds in a blue sky ...

I wish you could see this countryside now — green meadows pied yellow and white with buttercups and daisies, untidy orchards with their trees of blossom, misty pink and white, leaning over hedges, lark and cuckoo supplying occasional music, and lambs bleating in the fields. I keep rubbing my eyes because it all looks exactly as it should; and somehow it's the first time I've really seen a proper English spring in these four years ...

Day to day life is so absorbing one scarcely thinks that

117

there might be a time after the war. Do you ever think of it? And if you do, what sort of a life? I must say my vision of our family growing up in the peaceful precincts of some academic institution has rather paled in my imagination of late! I'm afraid if we're to be of any use to our age and generation we shall live strenuously all our lives, and perhaps be wanderers on the face of the earth as well — who knows? ...

How I wonder and wonder if you can be home about The Day ...

Meanwhile the huge events of the war flared and flickered as a background to all private plans and hopes.

On 24 June Honor wrote:

The Coral Sea, followed by Midway, must have been pretty serious blows to the Japs ...

The fall of Tobruk this week threatens our whole position in the Middle East, and our prestige generally. What is it that Rommel and his boys have got that we haven't? ... This week's National News Letter is very good — says that statesmen of the future, distracted by the complexity of peace-making, will look back with a kind of nostalgia to the days when it was simply a matter of winning the war! I don't think they mean to underestimate the latter task either.

1 July. I wonder where you are and what you are doing. Mails have been so delayed lately. As you say, you do seem so far away when there's so little data to go on, and no familiar background.

Oh when shall we three meet again? I'm beginning to think that all my thoughts about you coming home were wishful ones ...

Have been thinking what it means to have children — to be twice vulnerable as well as twice blessed ..."

8 July. A letter from you at last! Three and a half weeks is

118

not so very long to be without a letter, but somehow it seems longer when for every day of three weeks you go in hope to find one in the old pigeonhole and there ain't none.

9 July. The day before The Day! To think that when he is sixty we could be eighty-seven — all old together ... Indeed we are together now, all three, in the great Christian family all over the world.

16 July. After a week of waiting and wondering, I felt desperate till I decided to cease thinking in terms of days and hours any more, and to give up all impatience and rebellion. Feeling quite happy now ...

Our son was born at noon on 20 July, and a cable reached my friends in New York that same evening. But twelve hours before, *Wastwater* had slipped her moorings at Pier Fourteen and headed out into the Atlantic Ocean on our longest voyage yet.

CHAPTER 17

CARIBBEAN ADVENTURE

"Escorting a floating dock? Just the two of us?" I digested the idea for a few moments.

"Some target, eh?"

"Yes," said the Captain. "They wished me good luck as I collected the sailing orders — in a rather meaningful way."

It was a sweltering summer afternoon as we followed *Buttermere* out through the East River, the towering heights of Manhattan on our port hand, Brooklyn to starboard. As we passed in succession under the great bridges, it seemed each time that our mast must touch. Then the shadow of the bridge, lying clean-cut on the water, would leap over our bow, ripple across deck and superstructure, and drop flat on to the water astern with an almost audible click, as we swept clear, with room and plenty to spare. The streets of up-town Manhattan came into view not thirty yards away, with sweating New Yorkers going about their business or staring idly at the two small warships, wearing the White Ensign, steaming purposefully through the middle of their city. Suddenly the watchful Bunts spotted Commander E, standing at the end of one street. As the Senior British Officer in charge of the trawlers in the US, he had come to see us on our way. As we passed, he semaphored "Good luck, *Wastwater*," standing in the glare of the sun, on the hot shimmering pavement.

Presently the city was left behind, the East River broadened out into Long Island Sound and we passed through one or two fleets of pleasure boats and yachts, tacking about in the breeze and sunshine. To me it already seemed an age since I had hung up the telephone receiver on Pier Fourteen, my last vain hope of the news I had waited for, and stepped aboard *Wastwater* five minutes before casting off. Before our mooring ropes could be secured to those familiar bollards again, we had several thousand sea miles to traverse, and an unpredictable job to do. The cable which might have set my mind at rest was beyond reach for another twelve days at least.

Into the unknown. December 1939

BBC news from home

HMS Wastwater
"You looked beautiful to us"

Army friend, Jones, author, depth charges

Our charge, the floating dock

Buttermere, *at speed*

Alongside, Santo Domingo

Columbus Castle, first in the New World

New York: Alf, Fifi, Bunts

The twins at Bermuda

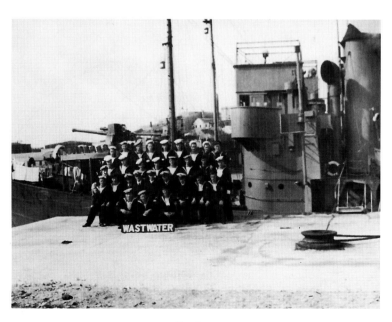

On show

Working rig

HALIFAX?
JUST AROUND THE
CORNER SIR!

Artist's impression, by Rattenbury

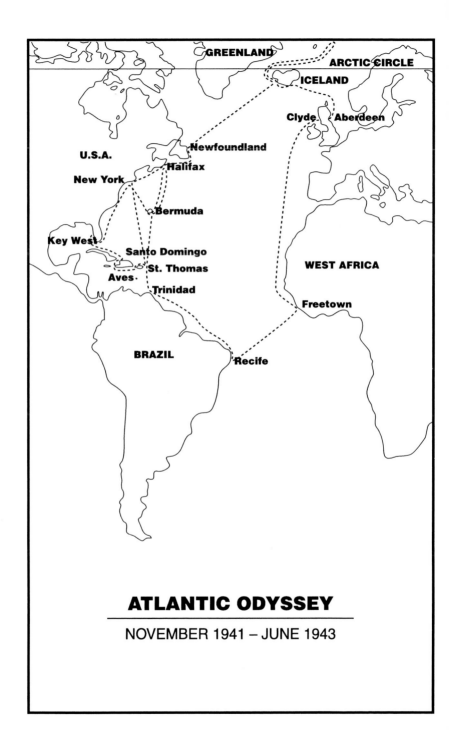

ATLANTIC ODYSSEY

NOVEMBER 1941 – JUNE 1943

Boat's crew, Brazil

Jack Wilson

Admiral's visit

Trinidad: Captain relaxing

First Lieutenant

Our first home; The Lodge, Tirley Garth

We came up with the dock and its tugs just at dusk, headed out of the Sound and set our course for St Thomas. An American Naval yacht (bound for Bermuda) joined us, going ahead of the tow, while *Buttermere* and ourselves took station on either beam, doing an irregular zig-zag.

In the following days we got to know the dock itself pretty well, watching it with anxious and incredulous eyes. Each dawn it seemed amazing that it was still there. Estimates of its size varied between St Paul's Cathedral and the Empire State Building. Built in America, it was destined for a British transatlantic base, that much we knew; our job was to get it safely to St Thomas, in the Virgin Islands. Two tugs, one American, one British, were towing, one ahead of the other. The dock itself was manned by a British Chief Petty Officer with a small crew; their main job was to operate the pumps (for in tow the dock made water continually) and to watch the towing hawsers. Through binoculars we could see them when off watch, sunbathing on the superstructure. But we did not envy them their roomy quarters.

One day melted into another and we crawled southwards.

Tuesday, second day out for St Thomas. A warm tropic day, a clear sky and a blue sea. Already we have seen flying fish, nautilus, porpoises and wonderful striped purply-blue fish swimming in perfect formation just ahead of our bow. The lads all fascinated, leaning over to watch, in minimum clothing. They have rigged up a salt-water shower on deck with a fire hose and one of the cook's colanders.

Felt restless last night, but fresher today. Weather much warmer and steamier. Sleeping on my settee for coolness. At this speed we would be a sitting target ... Have been looking at the plates of the ship's side in my cabin, just below water-line, wondering just how it might happen, and what I should do ... Almost certainly nothing I *could* do if we really caught a packet ...

Alf shaved off his Icelandic beard today — a loss to Broadway.

Third day out. Gnawing thoughts about Honor and the baby. Surely everything must be over now — but when, when would I know?

Meanwhile in far-away England Honor was praying that I would somehow know. That day in the notebook where I recorded thoughts which came in my daily time of listening, I wrote down, "All is well, and it's Peter". I felt strengthened. Then misgivings set in. Had I simply deluded myself? I had to wait three more weeks to discover.

> *Friday 28th.* Still the broad empty ocean — two passenger steamers passed to Eastward — all the shipping we have seen so far. Yacht left us yesterday for Bermuda — so now it is "just we two" with the dock — George is now Senior Officer Escorts. Still meeting thunderstorms, gulf weed, porpoises and flying fish — had one for lunch today — it landed in one of the boats, very tasty. Reclined a while in the hammock Jones has slung under the gun-platform. The lads doing much sunbathing — have to be chased to wear hats. Alf and Morrison making scrambling nets for the boats. Expect to make St Thomas Wednesday, or Thursday morning. Much dobeying going on on deck. Don't know when we shall see a laundry again. Today Capt. brought a bucket out on the boat deck and scrubbed away at some shirts.
>
> Saw some white stuff floating by today — Thinks I, ambergris! (Remembering Marvell's *Bermudas* poem and the "ambergris on shore") Fished some out with a boat hook, turned out to be raw wool — from some torpedoed ship, presumably.

The heat, as we crawled southward, was something new. Winter in Iceland, spring in New York, now summer in the Caribbean. *Wastwater* was designed to work in the Antarctic. Jones' cabin and mine, between engine-room and steering engine, were stifling. Incredible thought that we had once plugged that one ventilator with sacking! The wardroom had the stokehold on one side, on the other the galley, where the cook, sweating buckets, worked manfully. With the wind in a certain quarter, volumes of smoke billowed out and invaded the wardroom. On the door I inscribed Milton's description of Hell Gate: "So wide they stood, and like a furnace mouth, cast forth redounding smoke and ruddy flame." But the cook kept on.

The messdecks had been cleared of most of the beehive compartments, with our wind-sail proving a great boon, but even so they were crowded and stuffy. But it was the officers' WC, located above the conjunction of stokehold and galley stove, which became the most breathtaking inferno. "If I'm not out within five minutes," the Captain would say, his hand on the door knob, "send in for me."

Gradually we learned a new technique of life. After one or two sudden storms had soaked the messdeck with torrential drops, the seamen became canny in adjusting the guy-ropes of their windsail. The Captain, Jones and I learned how to perform gymnastic ablutions in the Captain's shower bath with a bucket of water (the shower mechanism still defied Chief's efforts). Our two small refrigerators sufficed at least to provide non-liquid butter and several days' fresh meat. But for all we could do, *Wastwater* in the tropics remained a hot steel box by day, and, at least below decks, a slightly slower oven by night.

But there were compensations, such as the pleasure of coming up for the night watches clad only in cotton shorts and shirt. At sea in wartime you must sleep with all the clothing you may need if you have to rush on deck and stay there at Action Stations, perhaps for hours. There is the recorded case of a Commanding Officer who, caught in his bath when the Alarm sounded, dashed on to the bridge stark naked and sank a submarine while in that state of nature.

Then there were the nights themselves, sometimes furry and black, with torrential showers and lightning like continuous gun-flashes all around the horizon; sometimes warm and husky, with a phosphorescent sea and a sky opulent with stars, against which our dark mast lifted and circled unceasingly.

Every evening at dusk I reinforced the lookouts on the bridge, and we carried out a meticulous search of the horizon before getting into our night station. The size of the dock made station-keeping fairly easy, even during darkness, but there was the uncomfortable thought of a periscope receiving equal assistance. The dock was such a wallowing, helpless moon-calf; we began to feel an affection for it, the sort of affection, perhaps, that a pair of sprightly hard-working tom-tits feel for the great sprawling young cuckoo who takes such advantage of their parental conscience.

The tugs were responsible for the navigation of the tow; but we, too, practised our sights and compared our daily Noon Position with theirs. It seemed a snail's progress, the way those crosses on the chart slowly crept down the parallel of longitude towards the dot marked "St Thomas". Both *Buttermere* and ourselves made several asdic contacts and alarms which proved "non-subs" on investigation.

Making a landfall after ten days at sea is always exciting and this, for most of us, would be our first sight of the West Indies. My thoughts went back through the centuries to another ship's company. This was the year 1492, when Columbus, in the *Santa Maria*, with *Pinta* and *Niña* in company, adventured through these very waters, to make his first landfall in the Bahamas, the discovery of the Western World.

The log of that voyage, written down by Bartholomew Las Casas, records most of the things we had seen: porpoises, floating weed, flying fish. It is a document full of touches common to seafaring experience in every age: the Admiral's concealed anxiety, which sometimes deflected his judgment ("Sept 21. Saw a whale, a sign of land, as they always keep near the coast"), the fallibility of Quartermasters ("Sept 6. The sailors steered badly, letting her fall away to the NE even to half a point; concerning this the Admiral many times rebuked them"), the hands bathing over the side in calm weather, the cloud which their desires turned into the looked-for land.

Martin Alonzo with his crew repeated GLORIA IN EX-
CELSIS DEO, as did the crew of the Admiral. Those on
board the *Niña* ascended the rigging, and all declared they
saw land. The Admiral also thought it was land ...

The actual sighting of land occurred fifteen days later. On this
occasion Columbus, prudent navigator and respected CO as he
was, showed a certain tactlessness, if it were nothing worse. A
seaman, one Rodrigo de Triana, sighted the land at two in the
morning, but the Admiral himself claimed the prize of 10,000
maradevis promised by his patrons, on the basis of an
unauthenticated light which he had professed to see at ten the
previous evening. When he awarded a silken doublet to Triana as
consolation prize, the worst suspicions of his men were aroused.

There was a curious parallel in the circumstances of our own
landfall. The Captain had promised a tot of rum to the first man
to see the light we were making for, supposedly visible for twenty
miles. At dusk, excitement was high. Numerous volunteer lookouts
thronged the lookout bridge. All glasses were pressed into use.
There were cries of:

"There it is, Sir! Just off the starboard bow ..."

"Where d'you say? Where is it?"

"Light flashing on the port bow, Sir."

"That's a star."

"No, below that, Sir, to the right a bit. Swear I saw it."

"I can't see anything ..."

Several times the Captain himself thought he caught a faint
flash; but each fresh report proved unconfirmed. Eventually
enthusiasm ebbed, the volunteers moved off to get their heads
down, and the Captain began to wonder whether our Noon
Position had been a bit out. Jones, who had the Middle Watch,
came up at midnight. Shortly afterwards, he spotted the light when
we were no more than six miles from it and carried off the
Captain's prize. Since he was Navigating Officer, suspicion reared
its ugly head. "Why of course," he protested, "the light's reduced
in power — only visible six miles now. I made a note of it on the

chart. See for yourself if you doubt me." Examination of the chart proved that the correction *had* been entered, but in pencil so extremely faint and unobtrusive that doubts were never finally laid to rest.

Our arrival at St Thomas was magical. I came up on watch at 4 am to find us steaming slowly through the strait between St Thomas and the next island. Ahead was a white triangular ghost, Sail Rock, with which a French warship had once fought a naval action.

It was a balmy night, with the gentlest of breezes, and the whole scene was drenched in moonlight. Our gun, as I looked from the bridge window, threw a clear-cut shadow on the matting of the gun-platform, and the dark shapes of the mountains on St Thomas loomed up just as I had pictured them from the chart. The stars overhead glimmered palely; we had reduced speed so as not to arrive before daylight, and we drifted on like dark shadows ourselves: we and *Buttermere*, the two tugs and the dock. And still the moonlight poured down, and the lighthouse flashed on our starboard beam, drawing slowly astern, and on the bridge barely a word was spoken. Soundlessly, imperceptibly, we entered the Caribbean.

As we rounded Sail Rock, daylight came and soon we were looking at the island of St Thomas from the south, the well-defined saddle of Signal Hill, the shoulder of Bluebeard Castle, the harbour entrance and the small town of Charlotte Amalie. Presently the signal station on shore began to wink, and our Aldis chattered in reply. We were to remain on patrol till the dock was safely anchored in protected water, and then proceed into harbour.

There was an unbelievable sense of relief among us: at the coming of daylight, at our own safe arrival, but above all, relief that the job we had been given had been accomplished, our part done, and the dock safely delivered. From now on, the responsibility was someone else's. Only now did we realise how much that responsibility had weighed on us, as a man discarding a heavy pack suddenly feels lighter than air.

Our relief was nothing to that of *Buttermere* and the tugs.

Once secured alongside, we all foregathered to compare notes.

"Talk about a close shave!"

"Yes, all round us most of the way."

"Don't know what the dock party must have been thinking!"

We discovered that for the last half of the journey, *Wastwater* had been guarding the wrong wireless wavelength. While the others were plotting U-boats reported in positions literally all around us, we had steamed on in unperturbed oblivion. At least we had aged less than the others since leaving New York.

This was our first experience of the pay-off from an event of which we knew nothing, an event known only to a strictly limited few, and so sensitive that it remained on the top-secret list for another thirty years.

On 8 May 1941, in the North Atlantic, *U-110* was depth-charged and brought to the surface. Her crew abandoned ship, jumping into the sea, believing their boat was sinking. It remained afloat, and a British boarding party captured the first complete Naval Enigma machine, with a full set of U-boat cyphers. The German survivors were picked up and taken below decks. The U-boat Captain, Lemp (the man who had sunk the liner *Athenia)* realised his mistake and tried to scramble back aboard his boat, but was shot dead. No knowledge of what had happened reached Germany.

This breakthrough played a decisive role in the Battle of the Atlantic. Clearly the Admiralty had been able to pinpoint the U-boats which sighted us, and perhaps to read their reports to U-boat Command.

Why had we not been attacked? Unknown to us, the U-boats had received instructions from Doenitz to keep their fourteen torpedoes for use against larger merchant ships, especially tankers. Or they may have been ordered not to attack the dock. In the latter case, U-boat Command made a correct decision. We heard later that the dock, escorted by an armed merchant cruiser, had run into very heavy weather in the South Atlantic, had broken up, and had been abandoned.

CHAPTER 18

SHOWING THE FLAG

Relieved of our charge, we headed for Key West, Florida.

First we had to escort a ship to Ciudad Trujillo, formerly Santo Domingo but now renamed, after himself, by the President and Generalissimo of the Dominican Republic, an "archetype of the old-fashioned Latin American despot", as John Gunther put it. The dictator had sided with the Allies and his only two ships had been sunk. The small tanker which we escorted brought desperately-needed diesel fuel, as the country was on the eve of a total blackout.

As we proceeded slowly up the river the town unfolded before our eyes. There were some imposing buildings. A huge national flag was floating over one lofty, turreted edifice, evidently a prison. High up we could see cells with vertical iron bars: behind them, watching us, were prisoners wearing shirts with horizontal stripes. The total effect resembled an irregular grid-iron.

"Libertymen who overstayed their leave," I said to my fo'c's'le party, who grinned a trifle uncertainly.

As we came abreast the modern concrete quay, it became clear that the whole town had turned out: a variegated throng eyeing us with intense but orderly interest. As we moved upstream, so the crowd moved with us. It was a little overwhelming. The pilot helped to explain. "The last British Navy ship was here in 1938, the Cruiser *Cumberland*."

The Captain stroked his chin nervously. *Wastwater* was — well, not quite a cruiser. Showing the flag had not previously been a big feature of our repertoire. As we slid alongside, police cleared an area on the quay about the length of the ship and established barricades. I began to get our gangway out, but before it was properly secured and was still wobbling perilously, important officials began to cross and jump aboard. Soon the whole foredeck seemed full of genial visitors saluting and shaking hands and wishing us well. Jones said afterwards that he had met the Chief of Police and the Chief of Secret Police who had followed the former to check up on him. But this was considered to be a fabrication.

In a lull I was approached by the pilot, requesting a small consideration for the men on the quay who had taken our mooring ropes. However, the general idea undoubtedly was that we were warmly welcomed to the city; we could not have asked for a more flattering reception. In the midst of it I had to clear the deck of a number of our hands who, unused to such courtesies, entirely forgot appearances and stood merely gaping.

Presently our first visitors departed and normality returned. The secretary of the British Legation arrived to find the Captain poring over KR & AI on "Ceremonies and Port Regulations". His duties as the Senior British Naval Officer in a foreign port perturbed him a little. But all was well. As the guest of the British Minister he was conducted on several official visits. We heard later of his impressive reception by the General, brother of the President, while a Guard of Honour played martial music in the courtyard outside; and of a banquet given by the British Minister, notable for its excellent wine and ceremonious hand-kissing, at which he met a number of eminent citizens and foreign dignitaries.

Jones and I, meanwhile, were entertained by Smithies, the Legation Secretary, who despite an acute petrol shortage motored us all over the town and then took us to dinner at his bungalow on the outskirts where we met his American wife and two small boys. We spent a pleasant evening sipping rum and coke, shooting at tins hung on the branches of a nearby mango tree and listening to Jones' Lancashire recitations. Smithies had also arranged swimming and a cinema show for our crew. Altogether Ciudad Trujillo had staged a royal reception for us.

The Dominican Republic comprised roughly two-thirds of the large, oblong island of Hispaniola, whose musical name was chosen by Stevenson for his schooner in *Treasure Island*. The Island was so named by Columbus who discovered it on his second voyage in 1494, when he also founded Santo Domingo, which is thus the oldest European city in the New World. The castle built by Columbus and later occupied by his brother, who came out as Governor of the new colony, still stands. Its walls were one side of the original harbour. The castle with its towers, battlements and embrasures might have been lifted straight out of a fifteenth-century Italian painting. Columbus himself lies buried in the Cathedral which, with the town square, was afterwards occupied by Drake for several weeks while he collected a levy and executed local notables who showed reluctance to disburse.

Naval discipline of the day is illustrated by the story of how Drake took the town. When he proposed to attack, one of his three ships hung back, considering the odds too long. Drake thereupon attacked and sank her, afterwards taking the town with his remaining two ships.

The architectural gem of the city was the ruined Franciscan Abbey and Monastery. As we walked among the venerable walls over turf floors open to the sky, I was reminded of Fountains Abbey, Rievaulx and others I had wandered through in far-away England (as it seemed, in another life). There were even the flights of pigeons feeding and building among the ruins (could they be Shakespeare's "temple-haunting martlets"?)

From Santo Domingo both Cortez and Pizzaro launched their world-changing expeditions. With their discoveries, the centre of gravity of the New World shifted westwards, but Santo Domingo still kept the name and prestige of a capital. It remained the seat of the Archbishop of the Indies. So much we gleaned in our rapid circuit of the city: enough to make us realise that this low-lying, white-walled Spanish-American town was the postern-gate between the Old World and the New.

The public and private buildings we saw had a clean, cared-for appearance; the ancient monuments were well preserved. All this was chiefly due to one man, President Trujillo, Generalissimo of the Armed Forces, Founder and Supreme Chief of the Partido Domenicana, Benefactor of the Fatherland, Restorer of Financial Independence, First Journalist of the Republic. He lived in great personal luxury and ruled the Republic with ruthlessness and efficiency. The local products of sugar, salt and matches found their chief markets in the USA and Britain. The Republic was at war with Germany and the President had donated land for a refugee colony, declaring his readiness to take up to 100,000 refugees. Many were already arriving, mostly Jewish, gratified to find a door not barred against them. It was unexpected and striking to be so confronted in one afternoon with the memorials of old European civilisation and the victims of modern European barbarism.

The final task for *Buttermere* and ourselves was to escort six merchant ships to Key West, Florida. The weather held fair and we had a comfortable passage. Nearing the Caribbean we turned up through the Windward Passage (a favourite U-boat hunting-ground) without sight or sound of the enemy, and steered along the north coast of Cuba.

The final morning dawned blue and sunny, the sea a flat calm. It must have been about a quarter to eight, because I had not been relieved of my morning watch, and a beguiling smell of frying bacon was floating up from the galley.

On the bridge we were watching through binoculars another convoy, nothing to do with us, far away on the northern horizon. In that early sunlight, every detail of the merchant ships and their small grey escorts was clearly visible. Suddenly, as we watched, from one of the merchant ships a white column of water shot up in the air, higher than her mast, and subsided. Moments later, the same with another merchant ship. Presently we felt two barely noticeable thuds in quick succession. That was all to tell us that two ships had been torpedoed. We saw the other merchant ships holding steadily on, the escorts moving to and fro in their desperate search for the attackers, and soon the two torpedoed ships had disappeared. In the immense area of sea and sky it seemed such a small, inconspicuous incident: it was hard to grasp that on the outcome of such sudden encounters the course of the war was depending.

Meanwhile, the sea lapped blue as ever, the gulls wheeled astern of us and we ploughed steadily, watchfully on with our own convoy, since there was nothing else we could do. In the morning we berthed at Key West and heard details. The two ships had sunk in a few minutes with their valuable cargoes and heavy loss of life.

Key West meant one thing for me, then and ever afterwards: the place where a helpful telephone operator got me through long distance to New York. Marge Evans, at the home of my faithful friends the Twitchells, relayed a cable from Honor telling rapturously of the safe arrival and progress of our son Peter.

The lads came in to the wardroom for a congratulatory drink; and the Captain and Jones, with our *Buttermere* friends, took me out to a roadhouse hotel for a celebratory dinner, where flowing cups (actually glasses) flowed more fully than my memory details. I made a speech about fatherhood which was mercifully consigned to oblivion. From this point on the Captain, whose son was already two years old, made the most of his seniority in this department of life. As photographs began to arrive, whenever in social gatherings enquiries about families were made he emulated an acquaintance who boasted, "He reached for his photo-wallet, but I beat him on the draw".

That night in Key West I rolled into my bunk and fell asleep with an overwhelming sense of gratitude and relief.

The experience of seeing the two ships sunk before our eyes in broad daylight was a sobering lesson. It broke through, briefly, our surface cheer, the professional nonchalance which was so much part of the Navy's tradition (exemplified in Admiral Beatty's remark at Jutland, when yet another of his battle-cruisers blew up under accurate German fire, "There seems to be something wrong with our damned ships today!") I had seen the same tradition in Coxswain Pitt's non-stop patter while the bombs were falling round us in Belfast. It was something British, not exclusively naval, illustrated in story after story of Londoners in the blitz.

But now, as we sat in the wardroom, Jones was uncharacteristically serious. He told more about his experience when, as a young signalman, his cruiser had been mined in the Channel. "I was asleep in my hammock when we hit the mine. First thing I knew was waking up in pitch darkness. I'd been blown right out of the messdeck through a doorway into the flat outside. I remember a lot of shouting and groaning, and a Petty Officer calling 'For Christ's sake don't strike a match'. That was right, of course. There might have been gas, cordite, or anything at all in that compartment, that would go up like a flash. Someone found a torch, and we realised where we were. The ship had keeled over about fifteen degrees by then, seemed like fifty. At first we thought the hatch had been battened down on us; that was a bad moment. Once a damaged compartment is battened down, it's not opened till you dock: might mean losing the ship otherwise. We got our shoulders to the hatch, pushed up, and it opened, thank God. We hauled ourselves through to the next deck, then they passed up the two injured men. It seemed ruddy miles groping along that alleyway to the next ladder — I passed one closed hatch — the Stoker POs' mess — didn't want to think much who might be down there. At last we got out onto the upper deck, crowded with all hands. Everyone was quite calm, and the parties were reporting and moving off all the time: messengers, damage control squads, and the stretcher parties. The injured men were laid out on the deck; a number of dead men had been hung over a life-line, like towels on a rail. There was not time to clean up the blood that hung down from them, like festoons. I was sent to the bridge with the other signalmen, and we had a lot of signalling to do to the escorting destroyers. We had a lot of casualties, as one of the magazines had gone up. People on the bridge had their legs broken by the force of the explosion. At daylight one of the destroyers came alongside and took off everyone except a volunteer party. I volunteered to stay because I was all right, wasn't married or anything, and they were short of signalmen. There was a hole in our bottom you could drive a railway engine through, but we didn't know that then, and we got her in. The weather held, that was the one thing that saved us. When we got to barracks I looked so well I had the dickens of a job persuading the Jaunty I was really entitled to Survivors' leave — till I suddenly passed out in front of him. Delayed shock or something, I suppose ..."

133

We were silent for a time, each thinking over his own experiences. I thought of the bomb hitting the Commodore's ship off Aberdeen, and the whole bridge structure going over the side bodily in a sheet of flame; of another merchant ship, her cargo of wheat ablaze and showing through rents and holes as though she were actually freighted with fire. And yet most of her crew escaped. There seemed no rule or reason in it: just pure chance as to where the bomb or torpedo might hit, and how. Tankers with light aviation spirit had been torpedoed and little damaged; others with heavy, less combustible crude oil had burst into one flame. Ships had been drilled with holes like railway tunnels and had steamed on. There was a cold-blooded courage about those merchant ship crews, steaming steadily, slowly on, with ships blowing up ahead, astern, all round them, in the blackest night and at high noon. And in the midst of horror: human comedy. Someone had told me of a keen young lookout, told to report everything he noticed without exception, shouting to the bridge, as a tanker 300 yards away blew up with the force of a volcano, "Explosion on the port bow, Sir".

The unbelievable, unpredictable force of high explosive: of an explosion ten feet below the surface which could lift a lookout from the wing of a bridge and toss him, arms and legs waving helplessly, higher than the mast.

Yes, they earned their danger money, the men of the Merchant Navy. *Wastwater* was a small target, she was manoeuvrable, and she had teeth. Unlike a lumbering merchant ship, she would have some chance of avoiding an approaching torpedo, and of giving her attacker something in return.

On the other hand she was small. When a big ship is hit, it may be some time before she goes down, time to get away boats and rafts, time to send an SOS and to fire distress rockets. And the difference of an hour or two in the water might be the difference between life and death. In high latitudes there is the cold of water near to freezing-point. In tropical waters there are the fish: we wished to see nothing of them. A subtropical latitude would be the best to choose; but in such matters the choice would not be ours.

"Suppose we did get a smack from a torpedo ..." I began; and then stopped, realising it was a foolish question, unanswerable and pointless. Our boats, rafts and life-belts were as ready as we could make them; if they were all smashed, some wreckage might float off as the ship went down, otherwise ...

"Well," said the Captain, standing up and feeling it was time to close the subject, "no doubt there might be something left; and then again, there mightn't. What's our noon position?"

Back in New York, familiar Pier Fourteen and the Delaware convoys; but not for long. The sands of our American sojourn were running out. The U-boats had shifted their hunting ground; and we had shown our capacity for more extended cruising. Before very long the Captain came back from 90 Church Street with news of a new job for us: a small convoy for Bermuda. *Buttermere* and ourselves, as usual now; sounded rather interesting.

Before we sailed from New York we lost Jones. The award of his "second ring" had brought with it a new appointment as First Lieutenant of an Admiralty trawler in Canada. Change and movement were the essence of service life in war. Yet this was for the Captain and me and all of us a moment of more than formal regret. Jones had been in the ship before either of us. He had shared our life in the compulsory intimacy of one small company, a partner of our best and worst moments in the eleven eventful months since we had sailed out of Aberdeen in November 1941. His irrepressible salty humour had often buoyed up our spirits; his shrewd sense and cool judgment had helped us in many a tight corner. We knew we should miss him greatly.

The ship's company subscribed generously to present him with a small clock, suitably engraved. There was the usual messdeck ceremony with much grinning, shuffling, and a "good luck" speech from the red, tongue-tied Cox'n.

Jones and I had a parting literary exchange. I was able to give him a copy of *The Jervis Bay and Other Poems*. In return I had the copy of *Newsweek* which had published his memorable ballad on the sinking of a U-boat by the Captain of one of the Staten to

Manhattan ferries.

He stood on Pier Fourteen as we pulled out, and waved, watching us gather way, heading down harbour as so often before. As we altered course, a corner of the shed hid his figure.

Though we did not know it, this was *Wastwater*'s farewell to New York. Had we known, it would have given added point to the news which the Captain brought back just before sailing, which was that *Buttermere* and ourselves had each been awarded the US Navy's official "Well Done" for our recent services. Evidently our successful arrival at St Thomas with the floating dock had occasioned others than ourselves a mixture of surprise and relief.

CHAPTER 19

THE REMOTE BERMUDAS

Before we sailed with a small convoy for Bermuda, our last job for the US Navy, the Captain called in at 90 Church Street to say farewell. Their regrets at losing us went beyond official formalities.

"They thanked both ships warmly," said the Captain, "for working so hard and for giving them no headaches". That, with the US Navy's official "Well done" for our escort of the dock to St Thomas, left a pleasant taste in our mouths as we said a final goodbye to the eastern seaboard of the USA.

In replacement for Jones we had picked up two new Sub-lieutenants: Rattenbury, a modest Dorset man with a quiet irony which proved a great asset; and Wilson, a cheerful, vigorous, enthusiastic New Zealander, who disclosed that he had been seasick crossing the Atlantic in the *Queen Mary*.

For me an aura of fascination had hung over the name Bermuda, ever since I had read at school the exquisite poem *Where the remote Bermudas ride* ... by Andrew Marvell, foreign secretary to Cromwell, MP for Hull and friend of Milton. I looked forward to seeing the tropical Paradise, lavish in God's natural gifts, described in the poem. I knew too that Shakespeare had drawn on reports of Bermuda in his picture of Prospero's magic isle in *The Tempest*.

As we moved up harbour we could clearly see the light sandy soil, the low dark green elm trees, and the white houses dotted here and there with a clean, windswept look.

> With cedars chosen by His hand
> From Lebanon, He stores the land ...

"Yes, they're cedars all right," the pilot told me. "Not tall though: very slow-growing, close-ringed. Good timber for boat building." The first English settlers in the island, after losing their ships in a gale, built a new vessel, largely from the local timber, and sailed in her the 600 miles to the North American coast.

"The Bermudas" is an accurate description, for there are many islands, some separated by only a few yards of shallow water and connected by a causeway. Their combined area is only twenty square miles. This string of islands lies in the shape of a half-curled crayfish, with the dockyard and Hamilton town forming the south-western claw. But the land above sea level is really only the projecting southern rim of a roughly circular table-top which may be the summit of a submerged volcano. The rest of the area consists of sandy reefs and shoals, sometimes no more than a few feet deep. All round the edges of the circle the ocean bottom falls steeply away to an average depth of three miles. The highest hill in the Bermudas is under 300 feet above sea level. It might seem to need only the slightest tremor of the earth's crust to sink those last precarious remnants of dry land beneath the waves.

With *Buttermere* we berthed by the white stone quay of the old British dockyard, in pre-war days the main dockyard for the West Indies station. It retained an indefinable flavour of the Nelsonian era: the square stone buildings, the emplacements for cannon, the derelict capstans on the jetties that once creaked and strained as heavy sailing ships were warped through the narrow entrance into the basin.

In spite of the busy American tourist trade, or perhaps because of it, the atmosphere of Bermuda remained totally British — or so at least it seemed to us, fresh from eight months in the United States. With few exceptions motor traffic was banned, and carriages were picturesque but expensive; so I hired a bicycle and explored the seventeen miles of winding tree-lined road which led to St George's, the eastern extremity of Bermuda.

In places the road was a cutting between high banks of rhododendrons, and the cedars almost met overhead. A dream seemed to brood over Bermuda. Stopping, I heard only the distant surf or the sighing of the wind in the branches. But the sea was everywhere, either the lovely harbour of Hamilton, with its miniature islands and bays, or the strong but still not savage ocean breaking along the outer beaches. With Marvell's lavish description in my mind, I had expected tropical luxuriance, but the climate and vegetation of Bermuda proved temperate rather than tropical. In secluded dells I saw men ploughing by white farm-houses that might have been in Cumberland.

After New York it was another world: the town of Hamilton with its faint air of genteel shabbiness, or the winding country roads with boards nailed askew to wayside trees announcing "Air Raid Warden" or "Stirrup Pump here". I hired my bicycle at a small shop from a black gentleman in middle life whose voice and manner were those of an educated Englishman. He had the grave courtesy of one who had no doubts about his status, no inward sense of inferiority to defend. He had, I learned, been a missionary in Africa to his own people, and intended to resume his work there when war conditions allowed. He knew England and we discovered that we had common acquaintances through a friend of my undergraduate days.

Our stay in Bermuda involved dry-docking and cleaning the ship's bottom of the growth of weed and barnacles which can reduce speed by several knots. Meanwhile we enjoyed the hospitality of wardroom and warrant officers' messes and of several Hamilton families. One of them had a son in the RAF, the other a son in England studying for Dartmouth. His father, whom we entertained on board, had, as an RNVR Lieutenant, com-manded a trawler in the last war.

Visiting the internationally famous Royal Bermuda Yacht Club, I saw on its walls a picture of the clipper *Flying Cloud* in which my grandmother, as a girl of seventeen, had sailed from the Clyde to Australia to be married. I could clearly remember her describing the pigs and hen coops on deck during her three months' lonely voyage.

The Captain and I also visited the new American Naval Base, part of the trade-off for the US World War I destroyers handed over to the RN. In view of the crowding in Bermuda, the resource-ful Americans had created land for both airfield and naval base by filling in part of the harbour and some shallow lakes.

As always, the base was equipped to the last detail: air

conditioning, filing cabinets, typewriters, Coca Cola machines. It had been prefabricated and shipped complete. The American policy of starting with convenient living and working conditions, and their success in narrowing the gap between planning and putting into effect, impressed us once again.

But everything in Bermuda was overshadowed by one fact: it was there that we heard the news. As I saw the Captain returning from his visit to Admiralty House to enquire about our future, something in his demeanour gave a forewarning.

"Well," he said, "We're off to South Africa."

As far as I was concerned, the disappointment was less sharp than on that previous occasion in Iceland, but more deadening: a kind of dull muffled greyness spreading over the whole horizon. I realised for the first time how much I had built unconsciously, irrationally, on the idea that our next move from America must be back to Britain. Now there was no perceptible limit to our exile save the end of the war. There was no next objective, no fixed point of hope, however remote, for our deepest thoughts and longings. South Africa? Nothing against it, except that from where we were it might as well be another planet or the end of the world. After the first shock I felt a conviction, again totally irrational, that we would never in fact see South Africa.

This was the moment when we began to see ourselves as pawns in a chess game in which we had no knowledge or control. We were like Odysseus after the fall of Troy on his interrupted journey back to Ithaca and the faithful Penelope. His wanderings were governed by the capricious, contentious gods and goddesses of Olympus, some helping, some opposing. We began to see similarities in our own situation. In a sanctum in the Admiralty we pictured a Power — X — single-minded and inflexible, with one aim: "Get those two ships to South Africa". But X was not all-powerful. Along the way there were various other authorities, able to deflect, modify, postpone the master-plan, at least for a time. All this against the changing strategies and needs of the war. This seemed a plausible explanation of our complex movements in the months that followed. In plain language, we surmised that each

Command we came under thought, "Aha, two useful little escorts, how *very* nice," and politely requested the Admiralty (not in so many words), "Please may we have the loan of *Wastwater* and *Buttermere* to do some small, rather pressing, jobs for us?" To which Admiralty (again not in so many words) would reply, "Well, just a teeny-weeny while," and then, after a suitable interval, "Time's up," and we would be packed off post-haste to the next destination.

Such a life had, for us, its grave disadvantages: uncertainty, isolation, a sense of being nobody's babies. On the other hand this nomadic existence brought a succession of interesting experiences and took us into a variety of strange ports such as few ships of our size can have visited in one cruise. And it meant that we stayed long enough in each place to see more than the waterfront, which is so often the limit of the seafarer's horizon.

The first episode was immediate.

CHAPTER 20

NOVA SCOTIAN NIGHTMARE

Sailing from Bermuda we turned north instead of south and took station on *Buttermere*'s port beam. It was breezy, bumpy and uncomfortable, and the glass was going down, but we did not guess what we were in for.

"While waiting for onward passage," the Captain explained, "they've given us the job of escorting a cable ship. We're relieving a corvette. Here's the position." The little dot on the chart was pretty well due north, roughly half way between Bermuda and Nova Scotia. "The cable ship's come from Halifax," he added.

I felt a flicker of interest. It would be something new at least to watch a cable ship at work in mid-ocean. I knew the fabulous prestige of cable ships for seamanship and pin-point navigation. But as the pitching and banging went on, with a warm oppressive atmosphere and a leaden hurrying sky, any anticipation quickly waned. Before dark I had the seaboats turned in and secured. No use risking them swung out. If the rolling got worse in the night we might lose them. I had seen a trawler which had kept her boat swung out too long. A heavy sea lifted the boat up, the next one filled it and tore it away as easily as plucking a child's toy; the steel davits, four inches thick, were bent down like a croquet hoops.

It was baked beans for supper again that night. Wilson was already being sick: the rest of us were feeling "quiet".

All next day we held on northward, all day the wind and sea increased, blowing from the north-west, all day *Wastwater* wallowed and wriggled and slithered towards that ringed dot on the chart, and from the bridge we watched *Buttermere,* now on top of a wave, rolling till we saw her bottom, now in the trough, only mast and funnel visible. We hadn't the stomach to make them a facetious signal.

By dark it was blowing full gale force, and the waves were already mountainous. We were rolling fiercely, spray was flying, and the bridge had the musty unpleasant smell of damp brass and leather. Worst of all, it had begun to rain, and soon visibility was down to a few hundred yards. With moderate weather, we should have reached the rendezvous at noon; but with this wind and sea slowing us up, we reckoned it was 7 pm and getting dusk by the time we got there. There was no sign of the cable ship; so George made us a signal.

"Intend altering course at midnight to steer reciprocal till daylight."

It was the best plan in the circumstances; but in that weather keeping contact at all was an almost superhuman job. We managed to cling on to *Buttermere* till 2300, then lost her in a squall. At midnight we altered course as ordered and steered the reciprocal, hoping to see her again at daylight, or perhaps the cable ship. All night we swung and plunged back, the only thing in sight the white crests of the waves which suddenly took shape out of the blackness, struck the ship's side, lifting her bodily, and went hissing away into the gloom.

Dawn came with greyness and rain and no abatement nor sign of *Buttermere*. We had in fact seen the last of her for that trip. Our rolling was now terrific: I noticed the straining anxious eyes of some of the younger men, and some of the old hands too. I wasn't feeling exactly happy myself. If a depth charge should break adrift, if a wave mightier than the rest should throw us over just a little further ... The Captain decided to come round and heave-to, heading straight up into the sea, going ahead just enough to give us steerage way. That felt more secure, but it was scarcely more comfortable. *Wastwater* was so short that she made a pig-rooting performance over each wave: up nose, down tail, steady — whoosh — there she goes, away under our keel hissing and boiling, and down we go into the trough. Now hold your horses, here comes the next one, even bigger.

Any earlier anticipations had entirely worn off by this time. We felt dull, dreary, lost and anxious. Next morning the sea seemed to moderate a little, enough for us to turn and steer for the cable ship's position once more, but all day we saw nothing, and by nightfall it was a full gale again. Ships could pass within a mile and not see each other.

Time, under such conditions, is meaningless; the mind cannot differentiate amid the interminable succession of watch, food, and sleep, the blackness of night being succeeded by a wet cheerless grey. I thought of Milton's lines about Hell.

> No light, but rather darkness visible
> Served only to discover sights of woe ...

One of those sights was the unfortunate Wilson. The second day out he relapsed into a chair in the Captain's cabin, where galley smells were less evident than in the wardroom, propping his foot against the washbasin. There he stayed for eight days, his only food an occasional ham sandwich administered by the steward. By the Log Book entries we were able to know how many days and nights had passed since we left Bermuda.

Our orders were to rendezvous with the cable ship, and our job was to act as her anti-submarine escorts. In this weather, any U-boat attack was most unlikely; but we could not be sure that the gale would not suddenly abate, when work on the cable could be resumed and our presence might be vital. So for the time being, we just had to hang on.

On the sixth day we received a signal that the cable ship had shifted her position a few miles north. We steered north, but still saw nothing. Our own charted position by this time might easily be miles out: there had been no chance of taking accurate sights since we sailed.

Whenever there was a peep of sun through the cloud the Captain and I would stumble on to the pitching, spray-drenched bridge with our sextants, prop our backs against something and make desperate efforts to align the rim of a dubious sun with a problematical horizon. Then, in the Captain's cabin, we would wrestle with tables and figures, while heavy books slithered and jumped about, and the paper got a spotty look after a time.

"Well, what do you get?"

"Well, mine was a lousy sight. I put us about here, roughly."

"Where? Oh ... well, mine was a rotten sight, too, anyway. Maybe we'll get a better chance later on." Pause. Nautical almanack slips to deck.

"You're probably right, you know."

"Me? Doubt it." Gloomy silence. Wilson goes out, comes back, relapses into chair again. And so on.

The situation was not lost upon the lads. Some cynic in the messdeck produced a new couplet to the tune of a then popular refrain. It went:

> Praise the Lord and pass the ammunition,
> Praise the Lord, and send a new Position ...

At last the weather did clear enough for us to get a reasonably good fix; and the same day came a signal that the cable ship had given up and was returning to Halifax. At last we were free to make for port. We made "Am proceeding Halifax" and set our course. There was no other possibility in any case. Wind and sea had gone round to south-west. Heading into it we would never have made Bermuda.

That day was the Captain's birthday. With the galley awash, pans flying round his head and working knee-deep in water, the wee Glasgow cook (who was strangely stimulated when contending with such difficulties) went to work, singing to himself.

> You're not to go walking down Lovers' Lane
> With any other bastard but me!

Miraculously he produced an excellent birthday cake, light as a feather. With the steward he brought it into the wardroom to be presented at tea-time. They joined the rest of us in chanting "Happy birthday, dear Captain". The steward also rose to heroic stature. He stepped into the wardroom carrying a tray, just as *Wastwater* gave a supreme lurch. His feet on the greasy deck slid away and he reclined flat on his back, holding in mid air the tray, still horizontal and unharmed.

As we set course for Halifax, the hurricane reached its peak. The next two days were without exception the worst weather I had ever seen, with wind the force we had known in Iceland and with hundreds of miles of open ocean this time where the seas could gather and build themselves to truly frightening size.

It was in fact the worst gale for twenty years, as we learned afterwards. Along the Nova Scotian coast piers were destroyed, small craft smashed and sunk, houses and buildings blown down. On the bridge the noise was ceaseless and stupendous: the banging of the anchors in the hawse-pipes, the keening of the wind in the standing rigging, an intermittent blustering roar as each new gust struck the funnel. Standing on *Wastwater*'s bridge you looked up to a mountainous wall of water, itself criss-crossed with intersecting lines and flurries, advancing with deliberate malevolence as though to crush this small impertinent vessel once and for all. Then it was that *Wastwater* showed what she was made of. When it seemed too late to escape, and the towering mass must come crashing down on us, up would go her stern, like the tail of a duck, while the mighty but ungainly monster passed under our keel, hissing and boiling in frustration, tossing and slapping and thumping us, but unable to destroy. Then it was that we thanked God for the skill of *Wastwater*'s designers and the excellence of the British craftsmen who built her. Apart from collision or running ashore, a ship may simply founder in heavy seas. We all knew of ships — trawlers, some of them — which had disappeared in weather like this, without trace.

How does it happen? There are many ways. The ship (particularly if the steering fails or the rudder is smashed) may "broach-to", and lie wallowing beam-on to the sea. Many a laden merchant ship, exposed to the fantastic force of the sea, has broken up in this way. She may get "pooped" — that is, when a sea coming over the stern forces the after end down. If flooding below decks follows (say through an open engine-room door) she may never lift her stern again, struggling like an insect whose hind-quarters have been squashed to the floor. Any structural flaw will show itself under the immense strains of such a hammering as we were getting. We knew of ships which had simply split along a line of welding, like a sausage cut in half down the middle. Another, slower way, is when the rivets start, hammered clean out by repeated blows, and the ship slowly floods — or she may simply capsize.

Wastwater was rolling as we had never seen her roll, 40 degrees and more each way, swinging and sliding and skidding. In the middle of it the Captain and I had an argument about stability: his thesis, as I remember, was how easily the centre of gravity may rise above the centre of buoyancy, thereby reversing the normal "righting" movement of the ship. At the height of the argument *Wastwater* gave a lurch which made us both cling on desperately, counting and waiting and wondering. By mutual consent the subject was postponed until our next spare day in harbour.

At the same time it got very cold, and flurries of snow appeared in the wind.

To keep warm I had to wear woollen underclothing, two pairs of trousers, two pairs of socks, boots, shirt, jersey, leather jerkin, monkey jacket, light oilskin, capok life jacket. For sleeping I discarded boots, oilskin and life jacket. That was stripping to the minimum.

At this worst point an extraordinary unexpected thing happened to the crew. The dull misery of the first few days gave place to an astonishing light-heartedness. They splashed about the flooded galley, dodged the spray on deck with shouts at one another's misfortune, and behaved like children at a party. Even Chief appeared on the bridge from time to time with a sort of sombre pleasure. Between deafening squalls, Lancashire Lewis was heard crooning to himself, as he operated the Asdic set: "Somebody's rocking my dream-boat."

It was I think, the exhilaration of that huge conflict, the zest of knowing that our lives and safeties were held in our own hands, that we were all fighting as one to conquer that elemental fury, and that the ship was fighting with us. It gave us a new confidence in ourselves, in one another and in the ship. We were facing the worst weather in the world and beating it. However wet, cold, tired and anxious, we were all, in an odd way, happier than we had ever been amid the relaxing amenities of New York. We had not sought this ordeal, and never would: quite the opposite. But somehow in the midst of conflict there was a peace springing from the fulfilment of a fundamental law of life: the law that man was never made to attain, but always to struggle and spend himself and partake in a titanic warfare whose outcome he may never see but which strangely gives meaning to existence.

Thus the cook, nursing a kettle of soup in his flooded clattering galley, sang at the top of his voice, "Roll, you bugger, roll!" and "Come along, lads, come and get it!", and the demoniac laughter of the sopping messman was whisked away on the gale.

As we ploughed northward, the cold became intense. It seemed an age we had been at sea. Unbelievable that we should ever enjoy the luxury of a sheltered harbour again. It became almost a feeling of physical hunger. We had been so long alone amid that tumultuous chaos that the real existence of land, of Nova Scotia, seemed incredible. At last, at four in the afternoon, later than we had expected, McIver on lookout reported land on the port bow. It was land all right, the bleak desolate coast of Nova Scotia. But it looked like paradise to us. The depth of water was decreasing all the time; presently the waves were smaller, with that brown silky look which means a shallow bottom with sand or mud.

Well, we had found the land. The next job was to find the entrance to Halifax harbour.

We had arrived out of the snow and sleet, after running two days on dead reckoning in a full gale. Presently we spotted a battered tower on shore: "Looks like this," I said, studying the *Atlantic Pilot,* "Old lighthouse on cliff". As we got nearer it looked more and more like the one described at the entrance to Halifax harbour. Presently we made out a conical buoy, and then a can buoy beyond, obviously marking a channel, and they seemed roughly in the position shown on the chart of Halifax.

"I don't seem to recall that shoal, though," said the Captain, pointing to some broken water on the starboard bow.

"Nor do I," I announced. "Best give it a wide berth." We did so, steering for the channel and the break in the grim coastline.

Passing the outer spit of land, we rode — amazing sensation — on an even keel. As we approached the first buoy, we were able to read its marking: "No 2 Buoy". That didn't seem right. Could it have been changed? Yet we were clearly in a channel of sorts.

"Ten fathoms," called McIver from forrard. Plenty of water, too. How very bleak and lonely was the harbour entrance: no sign of human life except a tiny lighthouse ahead on the shore. That didn't seem to be on the chart either.

"I don't believe this is Halifax!" burst out the Captain.

"Must be, Sir, surely. There's the western arm of water, and that's the wooded island ahead. We're all right." Providing reassurance to anxious Commanding Officers had become almost a professional habit with me. We went on for another minute.

"This isn't Halifax," said the Captain.

"Yes it is, Sir. Look, when we get to the end of this reach, round the next corner, you'll see Halifax right ahead."

We went on for another two minutes. That settled it. We couldn't see round the next corner because there wasn't one. It was a dead end. We had bolted into the wrong burrow; we weren't home yet.

"Hard-a-starboard, half-astern."

Grimly we turned short round and headed out to sea, retracing, with understandable care, the exact route by which we had entered. Fate had been merciful to us: we weren't going to leave any more to chance. We had clearly made our landfall well to the east of Halifax.

But out beyond the spit of land the blizzard struck us again with renewed force. It would be a beastly, anxious, and exhausting night out there: for we could never make Halifax in daylight now.

"What do you say?" queried the Captain, guessing my thoughts.

"I think so." We nodded agreement.

Round we turned again, and cautiously made our way into the harbour once more. By the diminutive lighthouse, in the shelter of a wooded hill running steeply down to the water's edge, we anchored in twelve fathoms. The blessed, unbelievable relief of that moment: the ship secure and still, in sheltered water, lying to her anchor, and the weight of responsibility for her safety eased from our shoulders for the first time in ten days. It had been like one long relentless watch. Now we suddenly felt at peace, and utterly exhausted. We made a signal to Halifax reporting our whereabouts and our expected time of arrival the next day. By now we had identified our sanctuary, Beaver Harbour, a small inlet in that indented coastline more than thirty miles to the north-east of Halifax. The force of the gale, and the violent swing of the ship with those mountainous seas on the quarter had combined to set us several degrees off our course, and the slope of the coast had magnified the error in our landfall.

"Well, anyway, we're here, and we're in one piece," said the Captain. "We've enough to be thankful for."

After a leisurely luxurious meal (those excellent baked beans!) at which even Wilson was able to snatch a little timid enjoyment once more, we lowered a boat and pulled across towards the small lighthouse, where a lonely figure had been seen chopping wood. But the rock ledges made landing too dangerous. We flashed a signal-lamp towards a lighted window, which promptly went out.

"He's under the bed," someone suggested. We pulled back to the ship again. Perhaps the lighthouse keeper thought we were a German landing party. There had been reports of U-boats. Rattenbury suggested that the lighthouse would report us to Head-office in their next Quarterly Return.

How delectable that night to change into pyjamas and stretch at ease between the blankets! Into my mind flowed that unforget-table line from Spenser's *The Faerie Queene:* "Sleep after toil, port after stormy seas", spoken, strangely enough, by Death. After Beaver Harbour, that line had for me a depth and resonance unknown before.

Soon a slumber like death reigned in cabin and messdeck, though overhead a cold moon looked from windy heavens on the ship and the shining water, while on shore the snow-powdered firs and maples crowded to the brink, and from his darkened window the lighthouse-keeper peered apprehensively.

Halifax at last! It had been a battering, pounding passage from our overnight anchorage, driving straight into the seas, with sheets of spray continually shooting right over the bridge. Halifax: and there was *Buttermere*, anchored ahead of us. She had arrived the previous day, having found and then lost the cable ship, which had thus returned to harbour alone. But such weather invalidated all normal considerations.

The Captain returned with relief next morning from reporting to Operations, having been prepared for a "bottle" over our detour.

"Not a word said. In fact they seemed pleasantly surprised that we'd got here at all."

He also learned that we were being kept at Halifax for further escorting of the cable ship. Could the roulette wheel be spinning again? We had no objection. Halifax was the western end of the direct route to Britain and home.

Best of all pleasures of Halifax was to see Jones again. He stepped aboard, large as life, from the trawler of which he was First Lieutenant and now temporary CO. During our stay he organised our social life down to the last detail, and left us only one regret, that we could not take him with us on our further wandering.

The gale had subsided, to be followed by the bitterest cold spell for years, reaching 20 degrees below zero. In harbour, with all ports and doors shut, with steam heaters at full power and a roaring fire in the galley next door, the wardroom ports never lost a three-inch crust of ice on the inside. Shifting alongside one day, the metal mouthpiece of my megaphone stuck to my lip, and had to be torn away. Unprotected ears felt as though they were freezing to a brittle fragility preparatory to dropping off. It was far colder than anything we had known in Iceland. No mild Gulf

Stream tempers the cold waters round Nova Scotia. Hence the surprising fact that Halifax, with the same latitude as Bilbao in Spain, is subject to these extremes of cold. Our small cabin aft remained chilly even though we kept the outer door shut, the steam heaters at full blast and stuffed sacking in the last remaining ventilator from the upper air.

The Captain and I visited the cable ship at her berth, discussed with her Captain our plans as escorts and our combined tactics in the event of attack, and were shown round the ship by the Chief Officer, a craggy veteran mariner who seemed to express in his person the meaning of such a phrase as "the finest tradition of British seamen". We discussed the gale.

"We saw you once," he said, and added, chuckling, "for a few seconds — on top of a wave."

The cable ship had an atmosphere of brass, teak and mahogany in the best and most solid tradition of British shipbuilding. The Cable Service is a service apart, generally regarded as the pick of jobs in the Merchant Navy. It requires precise navigation to find the breaks, perhaps in mid-ocean, and join them again. Cable ships have their own method of navigation, using deep water soundings. They know the ocean's bed as a surveyor knows the contours of dry land.

"Now just where you found us — would have found us," said the Chief Officer, "the cable runs over the crest of a steep mountain. Once we get contact with that mountain, we know where we are: the top of it is about 3,000 fathoms. Then we can start digging."

The actual distance along the cable where the break had occurred (whether through chafing, fish, enemy action, or any other cause) can be measured accurately by an electrical resistance. Once in position, the cable ship "fishes" for the cable-ends with grapnels and brings them both inboard for repair. The cable itself consists of a number of copper strands sheathed with rubber composition. We saw it stowed in huge tanks aboard the cable ship. To my surprise it was no thicker than ordinary garden hose.

The repair of submarine cable is ceaseless vital work in peace-time as in war. No service calls for a more versatile and yet specialised seamanship. Cable ships are few and valuable.

The Captain of the cable ship had decided that deep sea repairs were off for the winter season; so our next trip was coastal. It was very cold but calm, and the work could go ahead quickly. The cable ship lay stopped at her marker buoy, while *Buttermere* and ourselves patrolled round her, investigating any suspicious contacts and ready to attack with depth charges anything that might be a U-boat.

My imagination returned to those tanks of garden hose, which were in reality part of the three thousand miles of submarine cable linking America and Britain, carrying much of the traffic of communication vital to the coordination and direction of the war, coded messages between London and Washington, even secret exchanges between Churchill and Roosevelt.

Other messages also: at Halifax I found a cable, sent on by my New York friends. "Peter accidentally burned, my fault, out of danger, best attention, love Honor." I felt shocked and worried. If it was not life-threatening, was she blaming herself unduly? No telephone call was possible. With our uncertain ship movements, mail was unpredictable.

In fact it was weeks later that a letter brought details. Honor had left Peter, at four months, in an armchair by the unguarded fire. He had rolled, for the first time, and got his arm over the grate. It was a large burn. As he sobbed and she flew to him, she had the instant thought: "Give him his feed". He took the breast and fed. The doctor, who arrived some time later, said this might well have saved his life by warding off shock.

Halifax was the port from which the *Jervis Bay* had sailed on her last voyage, and there I heard from my friend Lieutenant Commander Ted Watt of the Royal Canadian Navy, as I have described earlier, about the Convoy Conference he had attended when Captain Fegen told the Merchant Captains exactly what he would do if they should meet a German battleship.

Despite the cold, Halifax began to feel home-like, familiar, almost cosy. Christmas preparations were considered. Perhaps we had been reassigned for regular work with the cable ship.

But we reckoned without X, that numinous power in some recess of the Admiralty, which caught and hustled us like autumn leaves out of Halifax, away and away southward on the relentless passage ordained for us.

"We're off," said the Captain. "0900 tomorrow. No defects to be undertaken, no nothing. Sail immediately."

As we passed Chewbuctoo Head under its mantle of snow the air temperature was still bitter and I was glad of the fur-lined cap and leather jerkin supplied by the Canadian Red Cross.

Next morning I ceremoniously discarded my long woollen underpants, which were no longer necessary. By evening the sea was calmer; I could relax during my watch that night. The following morning I changed into khaki shirt and trousers. The next afternoon Wilson and I were playing tennis in white shorts and shirts, in the mild whispering air of Bermuda.

But as in Halifax, so in Bermuda; the word had gone before us. X had been making the ether red-hot, and the cry was "Away, away," en route for South Africa. No non-vital defects to be dealt with, no nothing: instead, out, away, on. Like frothing hounded stags we sped out of Bermuda at 10 am on Christmas morning and turned south.

At this point, however, Chief took a hand in the game. Before we had gone far, a genuine main-engine defect came to light. There was no question of our repairing it at sea. By 5 pm we were back alongside the wall in the dockyard. So we could have our Christmas party after all. The next afternoon the dockyard was invaded by a lorry-load of assorted children belonging to our friends ashore. While we supplied tea to the parents in the wardroom, the children were turned over to the crew, to whose capable hands their entertainment could be entrusted. This kind of thing was no trouble at all to them. The seamen's mess had been scrubbed spotless and hung with a choice selection of paper bells, festoons, etc. The wardroom cupboard had been raided to rake up the necessary equipment of cups, plates, knives and forks, with the messdeck tables covered with new oilcloth and tastefully laid with a variety of Christmas fare which had been collected in Halifax. There were cakes, sweets, nuts, oranges and chocolate (then unobtainable in Bermuda) and a special fruit-studded jelly prepared by the cook. We had each contributed something from the wardroom, my contributions being some dried raisins from my Australian hamper and a tin of Australian peppermints, which were first prize in the Lucky Dip. After tea had unloosed tongues and energies, the ship was taken over, much as had happened at Staten Island. Small boys were evident everywhere, scaling ladders, rotating guns, ringing the telegraphs, shouting through voice-pipes; while their less adventurous sisters clustered round the Loud Hailer microphone. Presently, with much girlish giggling, treble voices chanting a parody of *Good King Wenceslas* were heard pealing out from our bridge, to the astonishment of the other ships in the harbour. When the time came for them all to go ashore there were scenes of vocal reluctance which, however trying to the parents, were undoubtedly flattering to the hosts.

Yet even as compared with the party in New York, something was lacking, not in the enthusiasm of our guests, but in ourselves. This was our second Christmas away and there was no visible prospect that next Christmas would find us any nearer home.

Putting our last-minute mail ashore, without hope of reply for many months, we let go from the basin, slipped down the channel and turned south for Trinidad. It was a warm golden evening with only the gentlest swell as we watched Bermuda, the "remote Bermudas", dwindle to a mere irregularity on the horizon and sink, as so many other lands had done, into the sea astern.

CHAPTER 21

THE ISLE OF AVÈS

This was the third day of our passage from Bermuda to Trinidad; yesterday we had passed from the outer ocean into the Caribbean by way of the Anegada passage, in sight of that notable graveyard of ships, Sombrero Rock. Now we were cruising along at an easy eleven knots over a sunlit, blue sea, delicately ruffled by a gentle West Indian breeze. I leaned from one of the bridge windows, enjoying its coolness for a few minutes. Then I went to the chart table again, to study our course and note any possible land which might be sighted during my watch. To the eastward were famous islands of the Leeward Group — Guadaloupe, Marie Galante and Dominica — mountainous too, but let's see, how far? Oh, no, too far off to be seen, even on a clear day like this. But to the west was this small island which we might possibly see: yes, it might just come within visibility, "Avès (or Bird Is.)", said the chart. Why, this was Avès! This island which we were approaching was none other than "The pleasant Isle of Avès, beside the Spanish Main!" I felt a surge of excitement and held on hard to the edge of the chart table. Only the solid back of the helmsman prevented me from giving vent to a shout of excitement, "The pleasant Isle of Avès!" How often it had floated through my boyhood imagination. In a moment I was back on the hearth-rug in our small sitting room at home, while my father read to us his own particular favourites among the stirring poems in *Lyra Heroica*. The "Spanish Main"! To me, in those days, large volumes could not express such a world of poetry and adventure as those two words! I made pictures and models of ships which I knew must have gone dipping among those shores; studied the technique of surprising mule-trains of bullion, of ballasting ships with doubloons, of overpowering astonished garrisons; I felt more capable of finding my way about Cartagena or Vera Cruz than about the humdrum suburb where we lived. And the hub and capital, as it were, of this enchanted realm was, thanks to Charles Kingsley, the Isle of Avès. Often in thought I was aboard one of the "... forty craft in Avès,

156

that were both swift and stout" and sailed in them against the cruel Spaniards and the avaricious merchant captains. My voice was heard in those enlightened and manly deliberations, where:

> A thousand men in Avès made laws so fair and free
> To choose their valiant captains and obey them loyally.

As for the natural surroundings, I moved among them as in a country at once familiar and entrancing.

> O the palms grew high in Avès and fruits that shone like
>   gold,
> And the colibris and parrots, they were gorgeous to
>   behold ...

While, in less strenuous moments, I knew what a delight it was

> ... to hear the landward breeze
> A-swing with good tobacco in a net between the trees,
> With a Negro lass to fan you, while you listened to the
>   roar
> Of the breakers on the reef outside, that never touched
>   the shore.

When the King's ships sailed on Avès, I felt a momentary pang at the dispersal of our buccaneering brotherhood, but it soon passed. So long as there were ships in the harbour, it mattered little if they were King's ships or no; so long as the round shot went whistling among the trees, and the crackle of small arms replied; as long as there were feats of seamanship and deeds of audacity by the shores and woods of those paradisal islands, then all was well upon the Spanish Main. And now I was ploughing through those very seas in a ship not much bigger than Drake's, on a course to pass within a few miles of the actual charted island. I came back to the present with the realization that the quartermaster was eight degrees off his course.

"South *ten* west, and keep on it. There's no excuse for wandering this weather."

On this course we should pass about seven — no, ten — miles off it. If there were hills, or even a peak, we might see it any time during the next half hour.

"Starboard lookout."

"Sir?"

"Keep a good watch for land on the horizon to starboard. There's an island there we might see."

"Aye, aye, Sir."

I studied the horizon myself. Nothing to be seen yet, but it was good visibility. I might yet see with my own eyes from our own ship the island that my boy's imagination had voyaged to and possessed so often.

I still felt a quickening of the pulse. These were, after all, waters traversed by Columbus and Drake, by Captain Kidd and Nelson: the hereditary home of adventurers, of men who had in sober fact ascended the Orinoco and climbed the peaks of Darien. And what of the real island of Avès? Kingsley, I knew, had visited other places in the West Indies and found the reality no less enthralling than the prospect. Could this actually be the tropic island of the imagination, where truth, for once, was no anti-climax?

The trouble was, it was touch and go if we would sight it at this distance. Dare I edge over a few degrees? No, we were keeping station on *Buttermere*, and I noticed that we were drawing ahead.

"140 revs."

"One four oh revs, Sir."

"Steer three degrees to port."

"Steer three degrees to port, Sir; course south seven west."

I was occupied for ten minutes or so in getting back into exact station: then there was some signalling and comparison of noon positions with *Buttermere*. The Asdic rating got me to put on the headphones and listen to his infernal machine, complaining of an

158

interfering buzz that didn't ought to be there; and the Captain called up the voicepipe for some information about the time of sunset and the prevailing tidal set we were likely to encounter during the night.

Altogether it was more than half an hour before I could study the horizon again. The lookout had seen nothing; and I realised with a pang that Avès must now be abaft the beam, drawing further and further astern. There was virtually no chance of our sighting it now, and that was that. I had missed what was, instinct told me, the moment which comes once in a lifetime and is not repeated. I looked with keen regret to the unbroken blue horizon beyond which, and only just beyond, lay the pleasant isle of Avès.

Only then did it occur to me that I had neglected one source of enlightenment which was to hand: the *West Indies Pilot*. These *Pilots* are standard works, published and revised by the Admiralty Hydrographic Department. They cover every mile of navigable water from Hudson Bay to the Antarctic, from the Behring Strait to the upper reaches of the Amazon, and they are a mine of information to the seafarer, supplying not only useful navigational data about buoys, lights, tides and weather, but also details of all sizeable ports, with port regulations, docking facilities, port resources and amenities. Normally the *Pilot* sticks to the waterfront, penetrating no further than is necessary to observe, say, that there is an excellent tram service, or that the climate is generally insalubrious for Europeans. When roused, however, by some particularly exciting subject, the *Pilot* is capable of launching into a paragraph or two on historical background, antiquities and local colour. Then phrases such as "a scene of great beauty" and "of great historical interest" may break through the general level of restraint, with their hint of subterranean fires kept under control. It was with the hope of some such rare gleam that I took down the *West Indies Pilot* and turned to Avès.

"To die is good," observed the Greek poet, "but better still is not to have been born." This is what I read:

Avès Is. (Bird Is.) (Br.)
Position 15 degrees 39' 20" N.
63 degrees 47' 00" W.
Area 3 sq.m.
Pop. Nil.

A bare rocky ledge occasionally visited by fishing boats
for the purpose of collecting sea-birds' eggs. Brackish
water said to be obtainable by digging. There are no
trees and vegetation is sparse.

That was all. It was enough. Straightening myself from the
chart table, I noted mechanically the bearing of *Buttermere*'s
funnel, now drawing slightly ahead. The breeze was fresher; her
bow was lifting more.

"145 revs."

"One four five revs, Sir." He was keeping a better course; just
about right there.

I closed the *West Indies Pilot* and replaced it on the shelf.
Then I looked out, with a sense of gladness rather than regret, to
the still clear horizon. Beneath it, just beneath, was the Isle of
Avès, Charles Kingsley's and mine. Still mine; and how nearly
lost. Soon it would be dusk, and there would be riding lights
aboard the pirate craft in the little bay that was never bereft of
shipping; where a perpetual spring of clear water gushed over the
warm sand, where the palm trees stirred continually in their sleep,
and the parrots and colibris flaunted themselves for ever.

CHAPTER 22

TRINIDAD AND A TOOTH

New Year's Day 1943, and the mountains of Venezuela taking purple shape ahead of us in the dawn light. We altered course to the eastward, and steered for the Bocas del Drago, those five mouths that lead from the Caribbean into the Gulf of Paria. Columbus gave them that name after nearly meeting disaster in the passage. The island itself he called Trinidad from the three hills which were his first landfall as he approached from the south-east.

As I looked from my study of the chart to those high-castled tropical islands standing like sentinels astride the Bocas, my mind went to Masefield's line,

> I have seen strange lands from under the arched white
> sails of ships

even though in our case it was only the drab grey curve of the windsail, trimmed to ventilate the seamen's messdeck.

Soon we were steaming through the narrow channel between precipitous walls that towered up many hundreds of feet, covered with green, matted vegetation almost within arm's reach. Then we were through, into the broad calm Parian Gulf, muddy with the silt of the Orinoco, and there ahead was the anchorage, with the capital, Port-of-Spain, behind it, and the hills rising to the conspicuous Church of Laventille. Acting on instructions from the shore signal station — they were ready for us — we threaded our way through the anchorage, full of merchant ships, crept cautiously alongside the quay, and made fast.

"Expect the unexpected" was a lesson we never seemed to learn. After the huge explosion of authoritative energy which had hustled us out of Halifax, out of Bermuda, three thousand miles due south in barely a week, we half expected to see a messenger running along the quay waving our sailing orders for the next stage.

"Better not send anyone ashore," the Captain said as he made

161

off to Operations. "We may have to sail immediately."

But it was not so. The imperious hurricane had either blown itself out or been deflected elsewhere for the time being.

"We have to wait here till some minesweepers arrive from the States, and go on with them to Brazil. Meanwhile we'll be doing some patrols round here."

As it turned out, we were six weeks in Trinidad, six interesting and relatively relaxing weeks. We had no objection to being kidnapped.

The Caribbean had been a rich hunting-ground for the U-boats, especially as the convoy system made the American east coast no longer profitable. We had seen the torpedoing of two ships near Key West. At one stage the U-boats were sinking a tanker a day. In August the haul had included five Brazilian ships, which had led to a declaration of war against Germany by Brazil, now our ally.

Our job in Trinidad was to patrol, mainly at night, to prevent U-boats getting through into the inland waters of the Parian Gulf and attacking the important anchorage. There was little for us to do except keep a good lookout and Asdic watch, and be always at the ready.

One night we had been ordered to do a patrol further down the coast, off some oil tanks on shore. It was suspected that a U-boat might have entered the Gulf that day and be planning a nocturnal attack. Suddenly the Asdic rating reported, "Echo bearing Green Three-oh, Sir". It sounded a pretty convincing one. Not worth taking any chances, anyway. "Ding-ding-ding!" went the alarm bells, and the action crews came stumbling up from below as we swung onto the bearing. The guns were manned and brought to bear.

"Depth charge rails and throwers ready, Sir," came from aft. "Very good, stand by."

We were going full speed for it now, closing the echo rapidly, poised to let go a shattering depth charge pattern on the marauder. The ship vibrated, excitement mounted: nearly over it now.

"Check fire!" yelled the Captain, who was peering ahead.

"You can ease down, now. There they go!"

At that instant I saw what we had been chasing and had mistaken (not unreasonably) for a U-boat: a silvery white patch in the dark water, a compact shoal of small fish swimming furiously away from us. As our bow clove through the middle of the shoal, they seemed to receive a fresh burst of energy, a sort of jet-propelled impulse, shooting off in all directions, like bursting fireworks. In that phosphorescent water it was an amazingly beautiful sight, like a white rosebud suddenly opening.

The days at anchor were a golden chance to get on with painting and innumerable jobs round the ship, which the Nova Scotia weather and our rapid passage had prevented. In conformity with *Buttermere*, we painted the ship in proper tropical shades: light grey superstructure, darker grey hull. The two Bunts applied themselves with zeal to painting outside and inside the bridge; the sea-boats were scrubbed and painted afresh; we even managed to paint out some store-rooms and the seamen's messdeck, which stimulated the stokers to like efforts. But the greatest metamorphosis of all was in the galley. In spite of repeated suggestions, threats and complaints, the galley had remained a plague-spot, dingy, grimy and greasy. The cook said "Aye, aye, Sir," and carried on as before, no wise distressed by this state of affairs. Now the initiative came from the crew. For two days we all lived on a cold diet, brewing tea in the engine room. The cook was turned out on deck, while a flying squad under my direction scraped and scrubbed the galley out from top to bottom with soap and caustic soda. Not a corner or cranny escaped. After that, in place of dingy grey it was painted out in fresh glossy colours: white for deckhead and sides with a light green skirting three feet up from deck level, and a neat black dividing line. Not only did the new paint lend itself to repeated washing; it betrayed each spot of dirt or grease as it occurred. When the cook was installed once more in his rejuvenated domain, he seemed a changed and chastened man. From that day the galley never looked back.

On deck the lads painted away, singing and ragging each other. They were all involved. Frequent pots of tea made the rounds; after all, there was nothing else to do out there.

In consequence we suffered a plague of cups and mugs left lying in odd nooks and corners. Threats and appeals were alike ineffective till Wilson hit on the plan of quickly collecting all cups found about the deck and locking them in the wardroom cupboard. After a few days of acute shortage, lamentation became loud; and when the cups were at length returned, the messmen saw to it that a bucket of water stood on deck, and that each man dropped his used cup into it.

These were days which brought to light the full merits of another new member of our company, Johnson, an Admiralty civilian storeman whom we had embarked at Bermuda for passage to Cape Town as a passenger. No description of him could have been more inept. In many ways he stepped into the shoes of Jones as a man-for-all-seasons. He ate with us in the wardroom, and in view of our crowded accommodation, slept on the narrow settee in my cabin. This made things somewhat congested, but Johnson shamed any idea of complaint on that score.

Polite, almost deferential, from the start he soon proved his usefulness. He repainted my cabin for me, sorted out the medicine chest and placed my Action Station boots ready every evening at sea, at the right angle for me to jump from my bunk straight into them. Soon, at our suggestion, he kept a watchful eye on our victualling arrangements, ordering as requisite in consultation with the Cook and the Coxswain. He designed a new ship's crest and collaborated with Rattenbury in embroidering a replica. Did the black line for the new painted galley require a specially steady brush? Johnson would do it. Was the wardroom fridge giving trouble? Send for Johnson; he would crawl underneath and fix it. His knowledge of First Aid later proved invaluable in the greatest crisis of our voyage. "Remarkable fellow, Johnson," said the Captain. "There's nothing he can't do."

Curious, I asked him where his versatile skills and unusual competence came from. He laughed. "From my Dad". His father had been a fitter in the Admiralty dockyard at Portland. As a boy, Johnson worked with his father in a workshop on the high crest of

Portland Bill. At the end of the day they would pack up and walk home down the steep descent. Only when they got to the bottom would his father say, "I noticed you left tools lying loose about the bench. Back you go. I don't want to see you till they're all put away tidy and ship-shape for the morning". Evidently the boy became a quick learner. Johnson was rapidly recognised as a valued new member of our company.

Some less welcome additions to our complement occurred in Trinidad. In the course of having some new wooden bunks installed in the messdeck, we acquired infestations of bed-bugs and giant cockroaches. The former we exterminated with a mixture of Lysol and paraffin; but the latter persisted, despite horrific slaughter by the steward. They seemed to have a special preference for the Captain's cabin.

Ashore it was hot and exhausting, though this was the cooler season. The waterfront where we lay, with the stores, repair sheds and all the paraphernalia of a Naval Base, was the most dusty, hot and tiring of all, after the manner of waterfronts. After ambling around the town once or twice and purchasing a few mementoes, the lads spent most of their time on board. As a sightseer the average sailor is easily satiated. However, we were able to arrange some outings through the good offices of the Port Amenities Officer, and these, which included lorry transport and crates of beer, were appreciated. One trip was to the bathing place at Staubles, another to the beach at Manzanilla, where they bathed in the ocean surf and climbed palms for coconuts. A third trip, to Maracas on the mountainous north coast, necessitated a climb on foot over a steep ridge, where the Amenities Officer, for all his sixty-two years, won their surprised admiration by leaving them all behind, toiling and breathless.

As for the Captain and myself, our stay in Trinidad was transformed by an almost chance remark in a letter I had received months before from my old headmaster, Jim Darling, in Australia. "If you should ever happen to find yourselves in those parts, do look up my friends the Whartons — I know they will give you a great welcome."

Our first evening in Trinidad found us sitting on their veranda (called a "gallery" locally) looking out at the restful green hillside, talking with delight of England and Australia and friends we both knew well. That evening was the first of many. The Captain and I, coming up from the dusty waterfront round the edge of the Savannah, would feel suddenly refreshed by the cooler air of St Anne's and the prospect of the witty, charming and congenial company of Louis and Hilda Wharton.

Through their generous expenditure of petrol and irreplaceable tyres, we saw much of the island. And what a fulfilment. All that Kingsley and Marvell had depicted in their verses of a tropical paradise and its lavish abundance now seemed realised in Trinidad.

Marvell had written of God's bounty to the immigrants in Bermuda:

> He gave us this eternal Spring
> Which here enamels everything
> And sends the fowls to us in care
> On daily visits through the air:
> He hangs in shades the orange bright
> Like golden lamps in a green night ...
> He makes the figs our mouths to meet
> And throws the melons at our feet;
> But apples plants of such a price
> No tree could ever bear them twice ...

(Perhaps a reference to pineapples, which I had seen growing in my native Queensland.)

We bathed with Louis and Hilda at the delicious sandy cove of Maqueripe, while portly pelicans skimmed over our heads. On a mountain road Hilda stopped the car while Rattenbury and Johnson climbed one of the thousands of grapefruit trees growing wild amid the competing vegetation, and threw down the golden fruit to us below.

When we commended the excellence of Trinidad grapefruit,

Louis arranged for us to be supplied with enough grapefruit to last the whole ship's company for a fortnight. In this way grapefruit supplemented, though it never supplanted, King Duff. That, with the daily juice of fresh limes, was our dietary concession to the tropics. But at the Whartons' table we partook of many new and colourful dishes: land crabs, which tasted delicious, even after we had seen them alive, clicking across the polished wood floor at phenomenal speed; breadfruit, uncommonly good when fried, sweet potatoes, oranges, pineapples, bananas, coconuts and many other things which were rarities to us, but commonplace to our hosts. In Trinidad the rare exotic fruits, the traffic of merchants from beyond the seas, were apples, probably wizened from cold storage, and gooseberries in tins.

In the northern mountains we saw the kind of tropical luxuriance which adventure writers love so well, the broad leaves of plantain and vines, where coloured birds rushed and flew across the road. In the valleys we drove through cocoa plantations, true "tunnels of green gloom", the leaves of the trees more sombre and lustrous than ivy.

With Hilda at the wheel, the Captain, Rattenbury and I drove the whole length of the island to visit Louis' brother, the manager of a coconut plantation at Cedros in the south-west. Running out through the straggling, ramshackle suburbs of Port-of-Spain (the native population in general preferred pianolas to house-repairs) we passed the site of the original Spanish capital, burned by Raleigh in 1595, on his way to explore the Orinoco in search of El Dorado. From there the road plunged among the reeds of the Caroni Swamp, reputedly the scene of black magic rites and eerie happenings after sundown.

The noise of the car disturbed ibis and flamingoes and all kinds of water fowl, who rose up like wreaths of smoke, flapping and protesting with scurrilous comments. Next came a belt of tall sugar cane, a prime cause of the early importation of African slaves into the West Indies. We passed the recently developed petroleum refineries, and climbed the hill into San Fernando. From there the road skirted the Gulf of Paria, among the sandy marshlands of the Oropuche lagoon, till it branched inland a little to the Lake of Pitch.

Onward again, through Claxton (the name an odd Anglo-Saxon shrub among the more flowery Spanish place-names), through a belt of dark entwined forest almost meeting overhead, to Cedros by Icacos point, to the house of Louis' brother in good time for tea. Cedros and Icacos! What more resounding, Argonautical names could anyone ask for? How Kingsley would have rolled them round his tongue with a boy's relish. Perhaps he did. Off the sandy beach by Los Gallos point, Columbus did in fact anchor and send his boats inshore for fresh water. He is said also to have abandoned an anchor there, but this is less certain. The number of anchors said to have been lost by Columbus in the West Indies roughly equals the number of rooms in England where Queen Bess is supposed to have slept.

Upon these sublime reflections obtruded a household crisis. Tommy, the house-boy, had declared a one-man strike. Most urgent: there was no domestic water, as he had not pumped it up from the well that day. Hilda was called upon to mediate, her brother-in-law being a bachelor. After a conclave with the housekeeper, a meeting was arranged in the back premises. We reclined on the verandah, while an indistinguishable murmur of voices came from the regions where the parley was taking place. Presently Hilda joined us, with an air of calm accomplishment; and the musical sound of pumping came from beneath the house. "He had no real grudge," she explained, "just a matter of simple male vanity. It's all settled now, I think."

Louis had been unable to accompany us to Cedros. As a barrister ("easily the best in the island," I was told privately) he had many demands on his time and had to be much in Court. One day, at our request, he arranged for us to visit the Court while a case was being tried. The Law Courts were substantial, on the pattern of innumerable English municipal buildings of the Victorian era. We climbed many steps and were ceremoniously conducted to our seats by an usher as black as ebony and immensely dignified. It was hot in the Court House, the complicated case was dragging somewhat, and even after a lively summing up by Louis, as Counsel for the Prosecution, I found I kept losing the thread of things. Nevertheless to us visitors the proceedings were oddly impressive.

In school history-books I had read traditional claims about British rule and "the benefits of impartial justice". The phrase had not meant much to me; but now I remembered it. A white man was appearing on charges which involved racial issues: he was interrogated by a white Counsel for the Prosecution and an Indian Counsel for the Defence (a benign man whose by-play with wig and pince-nez was unimpeachable) before a white judge and a jury which included several races and colours.

Because of the Whartons' generous hospitality those six weeks in Trinidad were more than a refreshing interlude, more than a fascinating exploration of a tropical island. For me they were a chance to glimpse the working of a West Indian community and a British colony at the beginning of its evolution towards independence. I was interested that the Colonial Office policy was to encourage the growth of trade unions, as a step towards responsibility and eventual self government.

The Whartons, though English-educated, had their roots in Trinidad. Their lives presented a remarkable illustration of British institutions and life amid a multi-racial colonial society in a tropical setting.

One night an Air Raid practice had been ordered. Hilda went to her post at a nearby Rest Centre. Louis was local Air Raid Warden. The Captain and I arrived at the house to find him seated at a table — local HQ — wearing his Oxford colours, and in complete control of the operations of his assorted Sub-Wardens. One was Transport (Fernandez, the local garage owner: "Capital fellow, Fernandez"), another Administration (rosters, watches, reliefs, etc.), while a couple of brawny black stretcher-bearers stood by. "All road traffic must stop. But, my dear fellow, you must *make* them stop. Yes, until the All Clear sounds. Now Fernandez, this telephone is cut. Go down to Area HQ and report ...". They heard and obeyed, with confidence. From his chair Louis organised them all, and they responded, because the human factor was present.

In the Whartons' sitting room, talking of books, friends, so many things we had in common, Britain did not seem so impossibly far away. We discussed the war, and what would happen when Montgomery and this American general, Eisenhower, joined forces. Things certainly had begun to look more hopeful; but the end of the war seemed as far away as ever, and Britain an ever-retreating mirage. Our delay in Trinidad had begun to revive our hopes of reprieve.

It was not to be. In Kingsley's poem the old buccaneer quotes Scripture:

But Scripture saith, an ending to all fine things must be.

The American minesweepers arrived, and our mission was to escort them on: south again to Pernambuco, Brazil, en route to South Africa. We sent off our mail into the void, but there was no hope of any in return for months ahead. It was all being diverted to Freetown, West Africa.

One glimmer broke through the darkness, a brief cable from Honor, stunning in its implications, and in the immense vistas of human advance which it suddenly opened before my eyes. That cable went far to redeem the pessimism of my world-view. It read: "All well stop first tooth".

CHAPTER 23

HOW WE FOUND SOUTH AMERICA

Our passage from Trinidad to Brazil was the longest — 2,600 miles — and also the loneliest of all our voyages. We had expected to travel in company with *Buttermere* and the minesweepers, but one of the latter was delayed for engine repairs, so we sailed independently. We sighted a distant convoy on the eighth day, but saw no land at all.

It was strange and a little eerie to be so totally alone in the ocean — no convoy, no dock, not even companionable *Buttermere* — and to know all the while that fifty to a hundred miles away, beneath the horizon on our starboard beam, was the coastline of the South American continent. We were totally self-dependent as we had never quite been before. Our two sextants, the standard compass into whose bowl we looked with the earnestness of crystal gazers, the charts spread out on the chart table: these were our only guarantees that we were not steaming on endlessly across the ocean until fuel, water and provisions gave out, leaving us becalmed and helpless. Not so much as a fishing boat, only ocean-going gulls, porpoises, a hazy sea and a pale blue sky.

As the days went by, we pencilled in our noon positions, creeping south and east in regular progression. Reason told me that we could not be far wrong, yet I felt a growing craving for some tangible proof, an increasing sympathy with the emotions of Columbus' men who, despite all assurances, despite their Admiral's subterfuge with the falsified log designed to conceal from them how far they had really sailed from Spain, nevertheless dreaded lest they should come at last to the very edge of the world, and topple over it.

As well, we had the feeling that we had said goodbye to our world. Bermuda and Trinidad had been British bases in British colonies; we had seen the strange as a background to the familiar. But Pernambuco in Brazil: none of us had much idea what we should find, nor any particular interest. Any change which was not in a homeward direction must be for the worse. It looked like

South Africa and "the duration". We were all a bit morose and laconic. The Captain and I were sorry to be leaving the congenial hospitality of our friends the Whartons. Wilson missed the company of a number of large New Zealand airmen he had discovered at the Air Base in Trinidad. Whenever they called for him, *Wastwater*, crowded at the best of times, had seemed about to burst her seams.

Crossing the line provided our first domestic celebration. The Navigational Oracles, the Captain and myself, decreed that this event took place at two-thirty one afternoon. There was no doubt that we were getting near the Equator. The Southern Cross had first been spotted by Morrison. Now, as we steered south and east, it stood higher above the horizon every night, while the Pole Star sank into the haze astern. On the day of our crossing, the Captain and I, endeavouring to take the sun's meridian altitude at noon had to chase its slippery image in our sextant glasses all round the horizon, for it was practically at the zenith. The next meridian altitude was easier. There was no doubt we had crossed into the southern hemisphere.

Wastwater's size and form precluded the usual pageantry of King Neptune's arrival over the bow. But for most of the hands this was their first crossing, and to omit all frivolity would have been unfitting. At the appointed time Lancashire Louis, hovering between suspicion and credulity, was shown through a telescope the Equator, a dark line on the horizon (uncommonly like the shadow of a cloud). Soon afterwards, with eyes glued to a stopwatch I fired six shots rapid from a revolver; we were officially on the Line. The two Bunts had organised the rest of the proceedings. From their eyrie on the Lookout Bridge they saw to it, with the aid of numerous buckets of water, that everyone appearing on deck was duly soused. The Captain and I attempted to escape by a simultaneous dash from either side of the bridge; but this sortie had been foreseen and provided for. Soon our shirts joined all the other garments fluttering to dry on the clothes-line by the forestay. The proper certificates were duly signed, and everyone felt immensely maritime.

For me it was a special moment. I had left behind the northern hemisphere, with my wife and son. I was now in the hemisphere in which I was born and grew up, under a night sky which my parents in Australia could look up to and recognise. I remembered my mother first explaining to me how to discover, from the Southern Cross and its pointers, exactly where due south was.

Crossing the outflow of the mighty Amazon, I was able to test the truth of a story which had long intrigued me: how shipwrecked mariners, adrift on a raft off that South American coast, found to their astonishment that they could drink the water over the side, for it was fresh. We put a bucket over the side, we dipped a cup, we tasted hopefully. The water was warm, blue, and very salt.

Soon Johnson again showed his sterling worth. On the fourth day Chief appeared with bad news. The main circulator pump had developed a serious defect. We would have to reduce speed to dead slow while repairs were attempted. It was an anxious situation. To reach Pernambuco would tax our fuel capacity to the utmost. Even when stopped, a ship must burn fuel to keep her dynamos and auxiliaries running. Time was certainly not on our side. Johnson again rose to the occasion. In conference with Chief, the plan was decided on. Thereafter, for two hours in the heat of the engine room, the two of them were the centre of a circle of helpers. Sounds of grinding, filing and hammering reached the upper deck, where the Captain paced anxiously while *Wastwater* crawled on, rolling and dipping, a sitting target for any prowling U-boats. "We'll never make Pernambuco at this rate," he muttered to me in an aside.

At last the exhausted heroes emerged, covered in oil and with a quiet glow of achievement.

"Reckon she'll do, while we get in," said Chief.

"Yes, I reckon she'll just about last it, Fred," said Johnson. Assisting an engine repair to one of HM Ships at sea was just another job to our remarkable passenger.

We were able to increase speed gradually to a little below our best. But it was going to mean increased fuel consumption from now on. There was not going to be any great margin for error in

173

getting to Pernambuco, and there was no nearer port where we could put in to refuel.

"We've just got to make it, that's all," said the Captain. We continued on at our most economical speed.

On the afternoon of the eighth day we saw a convoy, far away to the westward. It heartened us to see them — our first sight of anything but sea birds since leaving Trinidad — and to know that at least we weren't the only ship still afloat in the vast southern Atlantic.

Off the eastern shoulder of South America (as we reckoned) we altered course to skirt the coast southward. Still no land in sight. We could not expect to see it: we were too far off shore, keeping to the route given us. At daylight next morning we ought to be off Pernambuco, when we would alter course and steer due west for the coast.

During the night our reserve of fuel was depleted still further. The Asdic operator reported a contact which could not be ignored. We attacked with depth charges. No definite result, either way. But if a U-boat were there, damaged perhaps, we intended to be on the spot if it surfaced. For a couple of hours — as long as we dared in view of the situation — we searched and probed. Then, lacking further evidence, we had to resume our course. We had no safety margin left to play with.

At 0800 in the morning, a blue sunny morning, we altered course, and steered due west for Pernambuco. We had been running parallel with the coast all night.

"Even if our latitude is a bit out," said the Captain, "we're bound to pick up the land soon. I wonder how those fuel tanks are looking ..."

There was an atmosphere of suspense and tension throughout the whole ship. There were no hilarious shouts from below. The hands were keyed up, expectant. We had been more than eight days at sea, we had seen no other ship, save that distant convoy. Now we reckoned that at any moment we should sight land: a new continent, after nearly three thousand miles of unbroken ocean.

We held on westward, and saw nothing.

Half an hour.

"Hmm. I should have thought we'd have sighted land before now."

"Yes, Sir, so would I."

Three-quarters of an hour.

"Surely we can't be far off now. See anything, lookout?"

"No, Sir, nothing ahead."

An hour since we altered course.

"What the devil can have happened? It *must* be there, or are we all going crackers?"

I ran over in my mind every possible cause of error. Compass? But we had checked it carefully, and our observed positions confirmed that we had been steering the right course. Sextant errors? But the Captain and I had agreed pretty well with our sights this trip; we couldn't be very far wrong. And yet the land was not there. I glanced at the Captain. He had aged twenty years since yesterday: a deep furrow in his forehead, his face pinched and drawn. We looked at each other, hang-dog, appalled; guilty creatures, branded with an inexpiable crime. We had lost South America.

The sun was now high enough to take a longitude: the one remaining check on our position. Dully I fumbled with the catch of the sextant box.

"Lighthouse, right ahead!" called the lookout. It was Williams, our veteran three-badge AB whom I had had to punish for slackness two days before. His punishment was remitted on the spot. It was a lighthouse right enough, and comparatively close.

Presently we saw red cliffs, and identified them from the *Pilot* as Cape Aghostino. The explanation of our headache and heart failure was simple. A stream called the Equatorial Current crosses the Atlantic from Africa to South America, which it reaches at the most easterly shoulder. There it divides, one half flowing north-west, the other, called the Brazil Current, following the coast southwards. We had allowed a little, but not enough, for this current, which had set us further south than we expected, while a morning coastal haze had hidden the low-lying land, though visibility was clear enough to seaward. We had actually arrived about twelve miles south of Pernambuco: not a perfect landfall, but by no means discreditable after eight days' solitary ocean voyaging. Our celestial navigation was largely vindicated. Amid the bustle and jubilation, the lookout reported: "Tall buildings on shore, two points on the starboard bow."

It was a city, Pernambuco without doubt, glistening white in the morning sun, and we headed up for it. As we did so, Chief appeared on the bridge wearing his bird-of-ill-omen look.

"We'll 'ave to stop right away. Fuel tanks is bone-dry. I'm afraid o' losin' steam as she is. Come 'n' 'ave a look at 'em. They're dry."

There was no doubt about it, looking down through the manhole tops: there were the tank bottoms, clean and dry. The circulatory trouble, topped by our U-boat hunt during the night, had just tipped the balance. We lay rocking gently, within sight of the goal, helpless, unable to move. It was tantalising. We were too far off to get in touch by signal lamp and ask for assistance. We had accomplished the first 2,600 miles of our journey and the last twelve seemed likely to defeat us.

Then it was that Chief had his greatest triumph. Stowed at various points on the upper deck were several drums of lubricating oil, too large to be accommodated below. As First Lieutenant I loathed these drums with a deep loathing. They were bulky, unsightly, liable to break adrift and leave oil-stains on the deck. I had joined ceaseless warfare with Chief to reduce their number to a minimum. Now these abhorred drums were our salvation.

The "lube" oil, looking like golden syrup after the black treacly fuel oil, was poured into the tanks and sucked into the burners; the steam went up, the screw turned, *Wastwater* began to make way. If was rather like running a car on eau-de-Cologne, but it worked. Burning Chief's beloved drums of lube oil we arrived off Pernambuco. Signalling "I require to fuel immediately" we were berthed alongside the oiler in the harbour. Chief could not hide a certain sombre satisfaction but he was too good-natured to gloat long over his victory.

CHAPTER 24

VIVA BRAZIL

Pernambuco is properly the name of a state: one of the United States of Brazil.

The city which is its capital, where we had now arrived, is called Recife, from the reef which runs parallel with the shore for several miles, making a perfect natural breakwater for the harbour. The city was both picturesque and modern. A car arrived, and in rapid succession the Captain and I visited the British Consul and the Senior British Naval Officer, who supplied us with all necessary information about supplies, pay, mail, the usual leave to be granted, and a host of other things which new arrivals in a strange port need to discover speedily. The latter then took us to the US Navy Headquarters, where we learned what was immediately in store for us. It was an amusing repetition of previous experiences. As *Buttermere* and the minesweepers had had to put in to Belem, we were to wait for them. South Africa? No desperate haste, it would seem. Meanwhile, we could do some useful little jobs for our allies the Brazilian Government.

We lay alongside the quay in Recife, almost in the middle of the town, and it was hot. Life was made supportable by the South East Trade, which blew moderately and without pause. Without it the air would have been stifling.

We discovered that the city of Recife was built on a number of islands connected, as in Venice, by bridges. It was well laid out, with imposing buildings and a good tram service under British management, as were many public services and industries in Brazil. The shops surprised us, with their windows full of jewellery, watches, and materials of all kinds woven in Brazilian factories. There were many things on sale which had been rare in the war-time Britain we remembered. The Captain bought a tricycle, trusting that he would be able to deliver it before his son was too big for such things. To get back on board, he had to cross the deck of a US ship which was lying between *Wastwater* and the quay. As he did so, in pipe-smoking English dignity, with the tricycle tucked awkwardly under his arm, a friendly American voice was heard to enquire, "Say, Commander, when are you gorn to take off?"

Such shopping was new, worrying territory for me. I bought a rubber ball and one or two things which could be posted. At Bermuda I had put a hand-wound gramophone, bought in New York, aboard a landing-craft thought to be bound for Britain. But it never arrived, and later I heard that my gramophone had gone to take part in the landings at Sicily and Salerno. At Recife we were able to send mail — US Panair had numerous services throughout South America — but we could hope for none in reply. The ship, the sea, a shifting panorama of ports and coasts — these had become our life, these were the only reality. Sometimes it required a physical effort to realise that there had ever been anything else. Sometimes, to each one of us, recalling scenes at home in Britain in the individual everyday lives ashore we had left so far behind, came the thought, not as a detached philosophical speculation, but as a sudden serious question: did it ever really happen? In the hot strange foreign port of Recife we felt more isolated than ever from our own folk, from the progress of the war, from any sense of purpose or direction. We knew each other so well, the ship's routine had settled into such a regular round, we had been away so long. A sort of bored, irritable malaise seemed likely to settle on us.

The British community in Recife did all they could to help. We were invited to the Carnival Ball at the British Club, a magnificently lavish affair, with more lights than Piccadilly Circus in peace or Times Square. A number of the hands went, but most considered it too "high hat" for them. More popular was a series of athletic contests which we arranged against a British merchant ship which lay near us, SS *Empire Lobster*. The British Club made available their fine ground and changing rooms, and even provided sports clothes and the necessary gear.

At football we were defeated. *Empire Lobster*'s crew had had more time ashore than we and ran our punctured enthusiasts off their feet in spite of the stirring appeals of Wilson, who captained the team. The fever for physical fitness ran high after this. Each morning before breakfast we had Physical Training for all hands on the quay, with Wilson (who had once held Sergeant's rank in the New Zealand Army) as drill-master.

A number of small Brazilian boys would gather to watch this display of Anglo-Saxon heartiness, jumping in mimicry until chased away behind a warehouse. Whether as a result of this training or not, we roundly defeated *Empire Lobster* at cricket the following week, Wilson scoring a goodly sixty, and the whole team acquitting themselves gloriously. There was rejoicing in Israel's tents that night, but among the hosts of Midian, wailing and gnashing of teeth.

The athletics sports contest which followed called for the participation of the whole ship's company, except a reduced "watch aboard" and the Captain, who had to sit with the official party. It was a heroic searching day. I found that 100 yards, which I used to consider too short for me when university sprint champion, was now too long by approximately 70 yards. This was partly redeemed when Chief and I won the Siamese Race in convincing style by a system of counting revs and steering by selected leading marks on the edge of the ground. The cook did well in the sack-race (his head just visible) and the long jump was won by seaman Todd, one of our Liverpool Scouses. Rattenbury and Johnson were our chief hopes for the mile. Unfortunately they finished an easy third and fourth, quite convinced that they had another lap to run. In the excitement the judges had lost count, and the bell-ringer became quite indiscriminate: the point was never finally settled. *Empire Lobster* won the day on total points, but everyone was happy, and Chief and I chose to regard the Siamese Race as the only event of real significance.

Diplomatic courtesies were not neglected during our stay in Brazilian waters. Apart from any larger considerations it was undoubtedly good for the ship's company. They had lost their original suspicion of anything that smelt of "Pusser Routine", and now enjoyed an occasional day of what Jones had called "playing Navies". In foreign ports they could now be counted on to enter into the spirit of things and to put on a good show. In Recife, after a preliminary visit from the CO of a Brazilian escort vessel, who had been Naval attaché in London and talked to us enthusiastically about Bayswater, the Captain invited the Brazilian Admiral to inspect the ship. That morning *Wastwater* palpitated, while messdecks were swept and scrubbed out with special care, lockers and bunks tidied, and everything on the upper deck given an extra "squaring off". Then all hands had to get cleaned up and shift into their best white rig, while the sweepers, giving the messdecks a final wipe-over, execrated any clumsy sod who put his flat feet on a piece of newly scrubbed deck. Just in time we got them all out on to the quay, properly "fell in", as the Admiral's car was seen approaching, and smart they looked in their whites. Wilson called them to attention in his best Gunner's Mate voice and the Admiral walked down the lines with a courteous dignity while the Captain and I hovered. The Admiral was piped on board in good style by Williams (whose years of experience as a Naval quartermaster were useful on such occasions). After inspecting the ship — better seen when cleared of most of its inhabitants — the Admiral spent half an hour in the wardroom, talking pleasantly with us in fluent English about naval matters (the Brazilian Navy had a number of British-built ships), and inscribed in our Log Book an expression of his regard for small ships in the hard work they are called to do.

The sense of being on public view was galvanic. One Sunday we were invited to join a church service on board the US Depot Ship, a mile further down the dock. It was a hot morning; there was some disgruntled mumbling as our party fell in on the deserted quay. Despite Wilson's cheerful encouragement the marching as far as the first bridge was ragged and listless. There a few passers-by stopped to watch. Then a small crowd gathered at a street corner. Cameras clicked. The transformation was remarkable. Shoulders straightened, arms began to swing, the step livened of its own accord. As we passed some houses of dubious repute (as I learned) a few upper windows opened; a voice called "'allo, Baby". But our heroes marched right on, keeping perfect step, eyes firmly front, glancing neither to the right nor to the left. The heat and dust of the waterfront were ignored. From that point they were the British Navy, which knows how to march.

We visited Fernando Noronha, a small island belonging to Brazil a hundred miles off the eastern shoulder of South America. Our first job for the Brazilian Government was escorting a little coaster smaller than ourselves with troops for the island, which is both a penal settlement and a military post.

The Captain, with his usual flair for such gestures, invited the General in command of the Brazilian forces on the island to inspect the ship. The visit was arranged by Captain Rica, the General's aide-de-camp, whose English was at least better than our phrase-book Portuguese. The General, with his staff, came off in a smart launch, and was duly piped aboard. The staff were quite numerous, and *Wastwater*, even at anchor in the bay, was rolling appreciably. For half an hour her narrow unstable decks seemed full of large and even more unstable military figures, examining this and that, squeezing and clambering their way round our very restricted and awkward *lebensraum*.

The General himself was conscientious in inspecting all our armament. By virtue of my slight knowledge of Italian, which the General spoke, I was deputed as one of his guides. My laborious guesses at Italian equivalent terms left the General polite, but probably not much enlightened. However, he and his staff were at length wedged tightly but more safely into the wardroom. Goodwill flowed, and the General accepted the gift of a bottle of Haig as a small token of our friendship. The following day he reciprocated by inviting us (via Captain Rica) to inspect the coastal defences of the island, which proved to be considerable and clearly in excellent condition. We were rocketed about the dusty precipitous tracks in a staff car, visiting gun-sites, the air-strip, the fort-like prison for life-convicts, always under the shadow of the still-unclimbed Pico. After lunch at the officers' mess, we bathed at the General's private beach, where Wilson and I, as Antipodeans, were called upon to demonstrate the use of surf-boards, which our hosts possessed but did not fully understand. At

181

one point the Chief-of-Staff, struggling with a "dumping" breaker while his board slid idly up the beach, was heard exclaiming, "I cannot make it! I cannot make it!"

Finally we went with the General's party to witness sports and a football game, sitting in state beneath an awning while cooling drinks were brought on trays. One of the teams was white, the other from a black regiment. "The Africa Corps" explained the Chief-of-Staff. But the joke was without malice. Brazil, with its extremely mixed population, had virtually no colour bar.

The General recorded in our Log Book, in Portuguese, his "great pleasure in visiting the ship of His Britannic Majesty in defence of Democracy," adding (in English) "God Save the King!" On our departure we in turn made a signal (in English) expressing an appreciation of the friendship and hospitality we had been shown and concluding (a blind reckless leap into Portuguese) "Viva Brazil!"

Approaching Recife we discerned a small grey speck on the horizon. It got closer — a ship — no other than *Buttermere* arriving from Belem! In the flash of our linguistic experience we made, "Bom Dia, Amigo George, Com Esta?', spelled out and repeated ferociously by our Bunts and *Buttermere*'s.

"I can imagine old George cursing and scratching his head over that," chuckled the Captain, and sure enough something unprintable referring to "lingos" came back from the winking light of *Buttermere*'s bridge. Even when written out in fair hand on the signal pad, George's reply had a gruff North Country look.

Once alongside, we hastened aboard to hear their news. The sweepers had stayed at Belem. Another lot were expected soon; we would probably join them and go on in company.

The Recife *carnaval*, of which we saw several days and nights, was my first experience of a Latin American fiesta. It was an astonishing exhibition of that capacity for unselfconscious enjoyment which was one of the most engaging traits of the Brazilian people. Apart from the many Carnival Balls given by the various National Clubs, the public celebrations went on for days with a kind of fluctuating intensity. There were many processions and parades, but the festivities seemed to proceed without any special organization on anyone's part, by a sort of cheerful general will.

One evening the Captain and I strolled up to see the spectacle at close quarters, and wormed our way among the crowd thronging the main street. Everyone was gaily dressed, everyone had an air of excitement and expectation, they were crammed shoulder to shoulder, but there was surprisingly little noise. People talked but moved little, waiting. Then the band, on a triumphal car, burst suddenly into one of the rhythmic carnival tunes, written for the occasion, and with cries of delight the whole street began to dance. Everyone danced individually, not with partners, with a peculiar shuffle, holding one hand or both over their heads, swaying and turning to the quick urgent drum beats: old men, girls, little boys and grandmothers. There was no wild Bacchic abandon about it, rather a sense of absorption, of intense concentration. An hour of struggling through the ecstatic crowd exhausted us. We pushed our way to its outskirts, and escaped by streets deserted except for occasional children doing little solitary dances to the distant music. As we climbed back on board, the thump, thump of the drums and the brassy twang of the trumpets came floating to us on the hot Brazilian night air.

"How they keep it up," said the Captain, "is what beats me!"

He drowsed in the act of filling his pipe. I felt stolid and sleepy, and hoped the revelry would not come near enough to disturb me during the night. Were we getting old?

There were reminders that among the two million Germans and three million Italians in Brazil some would be dedicated to aiding the U-boat campaign of destruction against Allied shipping. An invitation to the "Officers and Men of the Allied Merchant Navies" to visit the British Country Club included a warning: "If you are asked: 'Your last port? What's your cargo? When do you sail? When did you arrive? What's your ship? Your next port?' The answer is, *DON'T KNOW*."

To me, sleeping again under the southern hemisphere canopy of stars, came a stark reminder of a war girdling the world. At the

British Consul's office in Recife I met an Australian woman, Margaret Mabberly-Smith, whose home was Geelong, Australia, and who was known to Honor's family. She was a nurse travelling to Britain when her ship was torpedoed in mid-Atlantic. She found herself in a crowded lifeboat and drifted under burning suns for forty days. She and a British officer were the only survivors. Despite equal sharing of water and provisions, all the rest of the boat's occupants, lascar seamen, had given up hope and died. The smile of the South Atlantic could be as deadly as the malice of the stormy North.

CHAPTER 25

SURVIVORS

"Two flat uneventful crossings of the Atlantic — it doesn't seem right."

"Touch wood," the Captain answered, thumbing his pipe. "We're not there yet. How much further is it?"

I measured off the distance on the chart.

"'Bout 390 miles. We should make Freetown on Tuesday morning. Those sweepers are certainly keeping good station."

We both looked astern to the four American-built mine-sweepers we were escorting from Recife to Freetown, perhaps further. Trim little ships, they cut the calm water of the South Atlantic like models on a manoeuvring board, their neat white bow-waves the only proof that they were really moving across that placid expanse. This was the sixth day out from Recife, the sixth day that we had steamed steadily on, watching the wide empty ocean and the four minesweepers and nothing else at all. They were almost as big as *Wastwater* but how small they looked at sea. Each day we compared our noon positions. With this weather and with five ships taking sights independently, the average ought to be pretty exact. To know your position with the greatest possible exactness is at all times a prime concern at sea. This trip it was to prove vital, in the literal meaning of the word.

We had been glad to leave Recife, not because we expected anything better of Freetown — quite the reverse — but because of the restlessness bred by our nomadic existence. At sea, all our thoughts were bent on the next port. In harbour, we soon found ourselves fretting to be away at sea again.

It had been a surprise to come without *Buttermere*. She would follow us but was out on another job when we sailed. We were to give anti-submarine protection to the minesweepers. The first day we exercised our agreed tactics to meet various types of attack. After that we settled down to the routine monotony of a glassy passage. At Freetown we hoped to get mail, but even this we preferred not to count on. So many things could happen: it was

185

best to be prepared for the worst. And after Freetown, southward to South Africa. It was four months since we had received mail: four months, four years, four centuries, it hardly seemed to make much difference. We felt more self-dependent, more isolated, than ever before in all our wanderings.

The future was wholly hidden, the past — our homes and Britain — so remote in time, in distance, in the throng of events and experiences we had been through since then, that it required an effort of the mind to remember exactly just how ... just what ... Or was that something we had read, or seen, or been told of? Our minds recoiled to the determinate present. When we crossed the line again the fourth day out, into the northern hemisphere, I noted the fact in the log with no sense of drama or excitement. We had got over that sort of thing.

Our course was roughly east-north-east, to cross the South Atlantic where it is narrowest, a mere 1,600 miles, from the north-east corner of South America to the nearest point on the great bulge of West Africa. Oceans and continents, they meant little to us now, so many entries in the Deck Log, so many pencil marks on the chart, so many days steaming on such and such a course, a new coast, a new harbour or anchorage, but the same *Wastwater*. We had almost come to agree with John McIver that "One place is much like another," because we looked at them with the same listless eyes.

"Signal just come through, Sir," said Bunts, handing me the pad. "General message. Sparks says he couldn't get the ship's name."

The signal read: "From SS ———— Torpedoed in Position —— North, —— West"

I called the Captain. We checked the position on the chart. It was about 70 miles from where we were, astern. We must have passed within 20 miles of it during the night; but we had seen and heard nothing.

It was an awkward quandary. Every natural impulse said "Go back". But our orders were to escort the minesweepers to Freetown. They could not turn back, their fuel would not allow it.

True, they would probably be all right by themselves: they were small, elusive game for a U-boat, and not defenceless. But if anything did happen to them in our absence we would be clearly responsible. And then there was our own fuel question. We should be all right for another three days' steaming if the weather held, but our scope was limited and Freetown was nearly 400 miles away. However, there was a ship in distress, and it was likely that we were the nearest help. Even this we could not be certain of. And "torpedoed" might indicate so many different things. Ships had been torpedoed and steamed on with speed hardy reduced; others had gone down in a few minutes with all hands. We didn't know for certain that the ship had been sunk or even abandoned. It was a leap in the dark either way.

The Captain decided to go back. *Wastwater* swung her blunt nose round through nearly 180 degrees, and we exchanged "Good luck" messages with the minesweepers. They wanted to come too, but it would have been folly. They ploughed on past us, heading for Africa.

We could not get to the position before dark, so reduced speed in order to arrive there at dawn. During the night we received a signal from Freetown telling us to investigate the torpedoing. The Captain's decision was thus confirmed; precious time and fuel had been saved.

In the night watch, as we swished through the darkness, I thought of all that could go wrong: an error in our position, in the torpedoed ship's position, in her hastily coded signal, in our reception or decoding of it. Any one of these wrong, and our search would be futile. Daylight came, and soon afterwards we entered a patch of oil which stretched for more than a mile in all directions: heavy fuel oil. Without doubt we had found the exact position of the torpedoing. Navigationally we could not have asked for more satisfactory results. A ship must have gone down, but there was no sign of boats or wreckage.

On Chief's computation of our remaining fuel, we reckoned we could afford that day for searching, but no more. We worked out a scheme of search, taking the oil patch as our centre, east, south, west, north, the last side of the figure taking us back on to our course for Freetown. That was the best we could do.

It was a clear blue lazy day, the gentlest catspaws of wind ruffling darker patches on the surface of the ocean. We doubled lookouts, visibility was ten miles; but we saw nothing. At eleven in the morning an aircraft was sighted, an RAF Flying Boat, far off, over the oil patch. That was good. They could cover many times the area of ocean we could, and we weren't alone in our search. Presently they saw us, and circling in, signalled "Have-you-seen-any-boats?" We answered "No. Am searching." The Flying Boat went off, and was soon over the horizon.

By 1 pm we were on our final course, still searching but less hopeful. "It looks as though they didn't manage to get away," mused the Captain. "She might have been an ammunition ship."

I was finishing lunch in the wardroom when I heard the drone of the Flying Boat in the distance. Rattenbury was on watch. The noise got louder, seemed to cross ahead. Then came a tremendous explosion that shook the ship from stem to stern. I jumped up, thinking, "Torpedo," and had got one foot over the door coaming when I heard Johnson yell, "That bloody plane's crashed!"

I looked and saw, a hundred yards off our bow, a huge column of water just falling back into the sea. Then some black wreckage, part of a wing, and some figures of men.

"Away life-boat!"

The hands on deck tumbled into the boat, hoarse with excitement. It was the work of a moment to lower away. "Slip!" The boat was in the water.

"Wilson in charge. Out of the boat, Johnson! Help Guthrie get the First Aid things ready." I joined the Captain on the bridge, and we slowly circled the wreckage.

From the wreckage a voice croaked, "Look out — depth charges!" Wilson steered straight on. There were three men on the wing. He got them into the boat, and searched the wreckage for more, but saw no sign.

"Come back," we yelled. As he pulled clear the wreckage began to sink.

The boat came alongside, we got the three airmen aboard, and laid them on the mattresses which Johnson and Guthrie had got ready on deck, under the awning. They were covered from head to foot in oil, blood and bruises. It was a moment I had dreaded from the beginning of the war, fearing that a close sight of mangled men would bring a paralysing weak sickness. From childhood I had shrunk from the sight of blood. But in the urgent need for action all that was forgotten.

"This is what the plane was signalling," said Bunts, thrusting at us a pad with the one word: "SURVIVORS".

"Yes, they found them," Wilson confirmed. "One said, 'we saw the boats'!"

"But where?" frowned the Captain. "Go down again, Number One, and see if any of them is conscious."

I knelt on the deck beside the Pilot Officer, whose eyes flickered, and asked as calmly as I could, "You found the boats? Can you tell me the course to steer?"

"Yes," he groaned, "men — two boats — course three-six-oh — no, wait a minute — " He made a huge effort. "Course one-eight-oh — about sixteen miles — "

He sank into unconsciousness. I left them in the care of Guthrie (our First Aid expert) and Johnson, and reported to the Captain.

One-eight-oh seemed the most likely of the two courses. We swung on to it, and rang down for Chief to give us his best. Three-six-oh, one-eight-oh, were going round in my head. But the decision was made.

As *Wastwater* trembled and churned her way southward, I gleaned a few more details. The great Flying Boat had approached, circling to signal us. After spelling out that one word, "Survivors", her nose suddenly went down and she dived into the sea, her depth charges evidently exploding as she did so. Of the nine men aboard her, three were blown clear. The three we picked up. The others must have been killed instantly. That one of those three was able to give us word of the boats, and a course to steer, was a miracle, a feat of sheer determination.

189

"Course 180 degrees, sixteen miles — we should see them about fifteen-thirty, Sir."

It was a perfect day, calm, with a clear blue sky, visibility ten miles. That was a mercy. But the sun was already declining.

"If we don't sight them before dark — " said the Captain, and stopped. I knew what was in his mind, the anguish of decision. But we would simply have to give up the search, or be becalmed, unable to make port for lack of fuel. Nightfall was our limit.

Volunteer lookouts crowded the lookout bridge; all telescopes and binoculars were pressed into use, raking the horizon for the tiny irregularities which would mean boats. As we had no crow's nest, Morrison climbed to the cross-trees, and lashed himself there. Yet none of the lookouts saw the boats.

This is how it happened, the Captain telling me the story afterwards. I had a sense that nothing more could be done; I believed we would find them. But he was torn by anxiety. By fifteen-thirty nothing had been seen. The distance might be more than sixteen miles, of course.

Sixteen hundred, and nothing in sight on the wide circle of ocean. Could one-eight-oh be the wrong course, after all? At sixteen-fifteen the Captain went on to the Lookout Bridge himself. At sixteen-thirty, having seen nothing, he came down to his cabin. He weighed and pondered the whole matter, the Pilot Officer's words, the course, our depleted fuel, the ebbing daylight, the men in the boats; and in an agony of mind he prayed that we should find them. Then he went on to the bridge and without telescope or binoculars looked out and saw the two boats. His sight was normally good, but not exceptional.

He came down and said quietly, "We think we have seen something."

I went up with him, and the boats were clearly visible, two of them, some distance apart. They had sails up, which were the two pinpricks on the horizon the Captain had sighted. We altered course towards them, and steered round in a wide circle in case the U-boat was lurking near. Suddenly there was a cry, "Periscope green two-oh!" There it was, between us and the boats, a white

190

ripple of foam. Bang! from our four-inch gun, then "Check, check!" Fortunately the shell ricocheted off the water, over the heads of the survivors, as we saw what had alarmed us. White smoke was blowing from a float dropped earlier by the Flying Boat. It looked exactly like a ripple of spray from a moving periscope.

We crept close to the boats, and stopped. There were more than sixty men in them; and the cheer they gave as we drew near was overwhelming, unforgettable, like something from the depths of the earth.

As the two boats pulled laboriously towards us with ragged oars, someone from our deck shouted, "Come on Cambridge — Oxford are close behind!"

The first man to step aboard was a tall figure in green silk pyjamas. It was Williams, the Captain's school friend, lately Secretary to the British Legation in Reykjavik, who had eaten his Boxing Day dinner fifteen months before in *Wastwater*'s ward-room. As they met on the bridge and shook hands, the comment "Dr Livingstone, I presume" was so obvious that nobody made it.

When the second boatload had been got aboard with minimum delay — it is never a pleasant feeling to lie stopped in mid-ocean — we set our course for Freetown, rang down for economical speed, and had time to take stock.

There were no sick or injured men among the sixty-three survivors: that was a mercy. While the tea kettle started on its round — which did not end till we touched Freetown, only pausing for replenishment in the galley — the Master of the torpedoed ship, Captain Mackie, SS *Celtic Star*, gave us a few more details.

"Three days out from Freetown he got us. Another twenty-four hours and I reckoned we'd be out of the danger zone, didn't I Chief?"

The Chief Engineer, tall, lean and sceptical, grunted assent. "Torpedo got her in the engine room," he said, "and I couldn't stop the ruddy engines. Spent four blasted days in Freetown getting the things to go, and then couldn't stop 'em when I wanted. She went down at Full Ahead."

Captain Mackie chuckled, "We could hear the Chief's cursing on the bridge. The rafts were gone as soon as we dropped 'em. We were lucky to get the boats away, and luckier to lose only three men — killed by the explosion. As we pulled away they gave her another torpedo. She didn't need it," he added wistfully.

"The U-boat came up to us in the boats — a big Eye-tie. They had lights on deck and were as pleased as Punch — walking about shaking hands with each other. They called us over and handed us Italian cigarettes, and said several times, "Remember, it was Italian sink you, not German". That was the last we saw of them. We separated the boats as far as we dared, and waited — I knew there was no hope of making the coast, and that Sparks had got away his signal with our position."

"Right on the spot, too," I answered. "We found the oil patch. You'd drifted south-east."

"Well, that was about all for a couple of days and nights, till we saw the Flying Boat, and then you! Talk about co-operation, it's marvellous."

We told them how nearly the Flying Boat tragedy had prevented that co-operation bearing fruit. By now Guthrie and Johnson had got the injured airmen washed and bandaged and laid out in the Wardroom, having shifted the table out on deck. They were all suffering from severe cuts and shock: one had a fractured hip. Johnson and Guthrie never left them all the way to Freetown.

Williams now came on the bridge, having discarded his green pyjamas for a khaki shirt and trousers which I had lent him.

"You fellows were lucky to be only two days in the boats," I said.

"Yes, very lucky," he answered. "In fact, you came just about in time."

I did not enquire further, but could guess the unspoken meaning.

He was on his way to join the British Legation in Buenos Aires. "After Iceland, they gave me time enough in England to get completely kitted up." He laughed. "And I was taking my books. I'm still half incredulous about the whole business. I keep saying,

'But this is *not* the sort of thing that happens to *me!*'" Ruefully he added, "All the same, I'm filing a patent when I get back: upholstered seats for ships' lifeboats!"

We weren't home and dry yet. Captain Mackie, a fatherly man, one of the old school of Merchant Captains, offered us the help of his younger officers in watch-keeping and navigating our way to Freetown. I overheard him telling them to put their backs into it and not let him down. Thereafter we never had less than three Officers of the Watch on the bridge at a time. All sextants were in continuous use, and positions came up from the wireless cabin, where the sights were being worked out in a continuous stream. *Wastwater* had never known such intensive navigation. Our guests' discovery of the difficulties under which we worked gave the Captain and myself much amusement. Our old-fashioned methods of navigation roused their barely-concealed disapproval; some surprise was caused when we arrived at a "noon position" within a couple of miles of theirs.

Our informality also surprised them. Several times, I caught Captain Mackie wagging his head in astonishment and murmuring "Well, well — well, well." Plainly *Wastwater* did not altogether square with the Merchant Navy's conception of life under the White Ensign. Yet somehow it worked. That surprised them too.

The night before we made Freetown, an incident occurred which almost finished poor Captain Mackie. Since picking up the survivors, the Captain and I had been on the bridge pretty continuously. *Wastwater* was crammed with humanity like a Thames pleasure steamer on Bank Holiday; in addition to our own company, we had the three airmen in the wardroom, and the sixty-three merchant seamen camped about all over the deck. The responsibility of getting our packed shipload safely to port had exhausted us more than we realised. It had been one anxiety on top of another. Suddenly out of the darkness Chief's face appeared like a gruesome ghoul.

"She's missing down below," he said. "Reckon oil's about finished."

The Captain and I looked at each other. Then, with one accord we burst into peals of laughter. This was too much: it was funny.

But to Captain Mackie, ignorant of all the antecedent circumstances, and schooled in a tradition of responsible seamanship, our reaction was frightening. I saw his startled eyes turned in our direction, and could almost read his anxious query: what kind of frivolous maniacs have we been delivered up to now?

As it turned out, the oil scare was due to a natural caution on Chief's part. By listing the ship we were able to continue, and even had a little to spare at the end of our passage.

Among the survivors was an elderly Army Sergeant on his way to the Falkland Islands garrison. He asked if he might shave, and I lent him the open razor I had used throughout our Atlantic peregrinations.

"Ah, now that *is* a good razor," he said, wiping it carefully.

"You prefer an open razor too?" I asked eagerly.

"Never use anything else, Sir, not if I can help it."

In a moment the torch of comradeship was lit, a charmed circle shone round us, enclosing all users of open razors, while beyond the pale, in the inferior darkness, stood all those who, whatever their other virtues, excluded themselves from our company by shaving with safety razors. Ten minutes' discussion on stropping, out there in mid ocean, and we had set the seal on our brotherhood, that Sergeant and I: it might even be termed our blood-brotherhood.

Among the survivors was the *Celtic Star*'s cook, who joined ours in the galley. By the second day appetites had returned and bread-making was decided on. Our cook was delighted with the tips he received. "Och, it's aye a matter of letting stand long enough," he exclaimed, gazing rapt, like Cortez in Darien, towards a vast new horizon. From then on his bread *was* appreciably better.

Keeping watch with the officers of the *Celtic Star* we heard more about their torpedoing. "It was my watch," said the Third Mate. "Had just had a cup of tea sent up — you do get dry in these latitudes. I saw the silvery track approaching, but it was too late to do anything. What I remember chiefly was the blast like a hot breath, and seeing my cap go spinning across the bridge. After that I was fully occupied getting my boat away."

It was clear that the *Celtic Star* had been a happy ship, under Captain Mackie's firm but fatherly rule. His officers were young and keen, and the Mate, Mr Pleasantry, managed them and the crew with an easy-going authority that sat lightly. They in turn were vastly curious about *Wastwater* and asked many questions, never having been aboard a whaler before.

"Of course, she was built for whaling in the Antarctic — hard work and no frills," I began. "She hasn't exactly the lines of a destroyer, and she's certainly no yacht." But they cut short my apologies. "As you came up to the boats," they said, "you looked beautiful to us."

We made our landfall off the Banana Islands in the morning watch, and at daylight entered the Sierra Leone river, at the mouth of which is Freetown. A launch with a Sick Berth party came alongside and took off the injured airmen, who were able to sit up by now. Johnson and Guthrie had presented them with a bill for their Lodgings, including "Fresh Air, Cockroaches, Delightful Sea View". They waved bravely to us, hating to leave the wardroom where they had been nursed back to life. Next a drifter came alongside and took off the survivors; we promised to meet them again when we could.

A light from the Signal Station began to flicker. Could it perhaps be congratulations, however unlooked for, on our achievement? We waited expectantly.

"Victualling Store Officer will call a.m. tomorrow, to muster your Loan Clothing," read Bunts. "Please grant him every facility."

After signalling our most urgent needs we secured to the buoy in mid-stream and slumped. *Wastwater* seemed suddenly empty and silent: uncanny. But oh, how good it was to rest, to relax into a blank, animal, delicious stupor.

Then the mail came aboard: six bulging sacks, all our mail for the past four months and more. It was a slaking of the drought such as we had known in Iceland, only many times more over-

195

whelming. We began sorting, and went on into the darkness. Everything on board save the barest essentials came to a full stop. What we could see of Freetown looked unappealing. We were exhausted after the strain of the last few days; the weather was humid and trying; the provisions had not arrived. But nobody cared. The mail had come and that was enough. Somewhere about 9 pm a box of ships biscuits was opened, and some tinned soup went round. Then we fell to reading our mail again, while the black tidal water swirled past the ship's side and distant lights gleamed in the anchorage and on shore, and we pored and pondered again those messages from another world, able to stir up in us such feelings of recollection, surprise, anguish, or delight. Riding at the buoy in Sierra Leone in the sweating West African night, we were like sleepers fumbling their way back to consciousness, or men whose memories were returning after long absence. We became ourselves again.

CHAPTER 26

WEST AFRICAN MIRACLE

Freetown is the capital of Sierra Leone, established in 1797 by the anti-slavery campaigners as a home for the freed slaves. It became a British colony and a naval base from which the British government could conduct its campaign against the slave trade. Now it was a base of vital importance in the battle of the Atlantic. The Admiral had his flag in the *Edinburgh Castle*, a former liner at permanent moorings in the crowded harbour. We secured to a buoy nearby. We went ashore rarely, to see our airmen in the hospital on the hill, our *Celtic Star* comrades in their quarters awaiting passage back to Britain, and to the bathing beach at Lumley. The climate was humid and enervating. However, there were many positives in our new situation. Once again *Wastwater* proved a lucky ship. The flood of mail had not brought to any of our company the kind of news which sends a man stumbling away on deck to struggle with his bitter grief alone while his mates drop their voices and look away in mute sympathy. And now at least we could hope for letters regularly.

"Ah, 's all right about the wife and kids," Chief reported. "Youngest is gettin' on OK. That bombin' gave 'em a shakin', that's all."

The Captain showed me, with complacent pride, the latest photographs of his son and approved my pictures with a certain technical appraisal.

Honor's letters brought accounts of our son Peter's progress, that mushroom growth of the first months. Even more astounding were the photographs, at which I gazed in secret with a kind of earnest incredulity, puzzled, like a monkey trying to get behind a mirror. To the Captain this sort of thing presented no special difficulties of comprehension. He had been a family man before we left Britain. But with me it was different. My son — it seemed altogether the most magnificent and satisfactory idea imaginable. But ... but ... like our friend Williams, I felt that obstinate query: "Does this sort of thing actually happen to me?" No longer two, but three of us. How would it be? Casually I began to sound out the Captain, from the depth of my profound inexperience.

"For a woman, having a child must be one of the most satisfying and fulfilling things — "

"Yes — " Pause. "But they get pretty tired and exhausted — need a break now and again."

I tucked away his words for the time — whenever it might be — that I might need to remember them.

Honor's letters (with certain gaps and blanks due to repeated redirection) covered most of the time since we had left America, a lifetime of wandering it seemed, though the ship's log testified that it was only four and a half months. In an hour or so of reading I lived through the experience and change of half a year of her life, six months which were momentous for the destiny of the world and no less eventful in our personal lives. The possibility of my going even further afield than the other side of the Atlantic had been a new blow, bringing with it all the accumulated weight of previous disappointments.

> I think I have a good idea what may be happening [she wrote in November] and you can imagine how I have felt. It does look like "the duration" this time, darling. I was just giving way completely to misery and self-pity the other day when Dorothy said (and she's the kindest person in the world), "you really are being selfish about it, you know". She helped me to see that feeling sorry for yourself is a kind of self-indulgence, and it was making me useless to everyone around me. Joan's brother has been killed in the African fighting. The news shamed me at my own regrets ...
>
> In all this time of separation, there's one thought that comforts me — apart we are learning so very much that we couldn't have learned together.

As I read I understood something of the extra burdens which the war had meant to so many women in the warring countries, the burden of responsibility for family decisions, of being "mother and father too". In our case, with parents and relatives far away in Australia, it could have been doubly difficult for her, doubly anxious for me. Then I felt a great tide of thankfulness that Britain, those islands where war had compelled us to make our home, had also given us friends who I knew would care for my wife and child as though they were among their own folk.

> Like you I live on one of those ceaselessly moving belts (what do they call them?) and it's the morning, and the evening, and another day, week, month, year.

But she came back to the thought which I sometimes accepted, sometimes rejected in bitterness and doubt:

> I do have the feeling that all this time we are apart God is working in us to fit us to be together again in a new sort of way — something beyond just "being together".

Arriving in Freetown, we had re-entered the British community. We listened to the BBC's African Service, we met officers fresh from home stations. After our foreign peregrinations, we had to re-acclimatise.

Professionally we had much to learn. There had been immense developments in anti-submarine warfare; our nomadic existence had tended to put us behindhand in these things. We threw ourselves gladly into the business of getting up to date. The Bunts spent their mornings with the Chief Yeoman of Signals in the Base Ship, furbishing their knowledge on points of signal procedure; they became severe critics of signalmen in other ships who made any slip.

"Incorrect Procedure," Bunts the Elder would mutter disgustedly, eyeing with all the punctiliousness of the newly enlightened some distant signal or flag. The Telegraphists went through a like professional wash-and-brush-up. Together with the Asdic ratings, I spent time at the Anti-Submarine School, learning the latest available tips on U-boat tactics and the counter-measures to be adopted. Wilson had new intricacies of naval victualling and store-keeping to master, while Rattenbury was kept busy correcting charts of our new area from pages of the latest navigational information.

Above all, we had to learn the teamwork of an escort group. We were not sorry to leave the sticky heat of Sierra Leone and get away to sea again, as one of the escorts of a large northbound convoy.

We were to work out of Freetown while awaiting *Buttermere*'s arrival from Recife. This news had caused us no flicker of surprise; in fact we now reckoned on such a reception. At least we could feel we were useful guests. Before we sailed, the Captain attended the conference of the captains of merchant ships and escorts, including the Commodore of the convoy and the Senior Officer of the escorts. He went a little in awe, but came back impressed.

"More plain common-sense than I've heard for a long time," was his comment. "And not too many orders, thank goodness."

It was warm calm weather as the great convoy, covering many miles of ocean, crept northward. From our place on the surrounding screen of escorts we could see the whole pattern. And what a difference there was since those early desperate days with the convoys west of Ireland, as I remembered them in the old *Northern Dawn*. These lumbering merchant ships were amazingly disciplined, the escorts were a team. Technical advances in such things as Asdic and Radar had altered the picture enormously. On the other hand, we in *Wastwater* had never encountered the U-boat "wolf-pack" tactics, which Doenitz had employed with deadly effect, and which for a time came ominously close to a German victory in the North Atlantic.

In the continuing see-saw struggle it was heartening to find how well the experience of many a convoy battle had been used to build the maximum co-ordination. In our instructions every possible contingency seemed to have been provided for; and the Senior Officer of the escort group exercised a free but firm discipline. One placid sunny morning Wilson on watch edged over from our station just a little to take a look at a brown-sailed Spanish fishing boat which we had sighted near the convoy's track. Repercussions were quick.

Wastwater from SO: "Just what is going on over there?"

SO from *Wastwater*: "I was investigating suspicious trawler".

Wastwater from SO: "Before future investigations, get my permission". Enterprising individualism was not good enough on a convoy screen.

During each afternoon the SO's Night Intentions signal would make its way by Aldis lamp from ship to ship of the escorts, while on all those escorts — destroyers, corvettes, trawlers — Commanding Officers would be finishing their tea and coming up to the bridge to study the dispositions for the night, with the position of the convoy and any expected changes of course. They would be looking at the weather, reckoning up wind force, the state of the sea, the duration of moonlight. And the Senior Officer, weighing all these factors and many more, would have to decide if, where, and from what quarter an attack was likely to develop, and dispose his forces accordingly.

It was an extraordinary thing, this coming of night, something you could feel through the whole convoy, and throughout your own ship. Before dusk the escorts began to move to their night stations. That might take some time, with a big convoy covering miles of ocean. During darkness signalling must be reduced to an absolute minimum; everything humanly possible must be decided beforehand. Then, with darkness, silence would settle, a silence not of tranquillity but of suspense. Smoking on deck must cease, all ships must run totally darkened. During the day there had been a certain amount of talking and noise, cheerful banter, a shouted instruction about keeping somebody's tea hot, the bang of a hatch grating carelessly closed. Now, unordered, all this stopped. The men off watch turned over to their reliefs in an undertone. The officer of the watch strained into the darkness, peering for the nearest merchant ship, or the next vessel. Things easy and effortless by day became pregnant with anxiety. Misjudgement is so easy at night. Most things happen then, and quickly. There might be the sudden red glow and following thump! of a torpedo; the flash of gunfire from the other side of the convoy (was that a depth charge?) or the sudden looming shape of a straggling merchant ship straying from her station. Whatever it was the night would multiply its terrors. Lines from *Macbeth* came back to me:

> Good things of day begin to droop and drowse
> And night's black agents to their preys do rouse ...

In the darkness you are aware of men watching, waiting, listening, while the great merchant ships crash on through the night like blind mammoths, and the smaller escorts feel their way like the outriders of the moving caravan. All through the night there is no relaxation, even under attack. A ship torpedoed drops out of line, astern, the rest hold on. They must. An escort pursuing the enemy must often break off and return to the screen rather than be lured too far. If the whole night passes (as most do) without incident, the tension and vigilance can never relax.

Then, with daylight, comes a miracle. To appreciate an English spring, it is necessary to endure the long rigidity of an English winter. To understand dawn at sea it is necessary to keep watch in convoy through the hours of darkness. It is not just the recession of danger. Attacks can happen by day as well as by night. It is the recovery of sight. At least you will be dealing with a visible crisis, a tangible foe. Actual danger may be greater, but you feel infinitely better with the first light. Spirits begin to rise. That second merchant ship clearly visible now, and the escort next astern is still there right enough.

"'S gettin' lighter, Sir."

The first remark breaks the ice, and as the stars begin to pale and a jug of hot sticky tea comes up on the bridge, a sense of lightness, almost frivolity, bubbles up in us. Someone down below is whistling; there is the clinking of cups and a smell of frying bacon floats up from the galley; the clock creeps on towards 0800 and "Watch relieved!" There may be days and weeks of voyaging ahead, the worst may be still to come. But for the moment we are capable of one sensation, and one only: thankfulness that the long night is over.

Back in Freetown we managed another visit to our airmen in the hospital ashore. They were all on the high road to recovery and assured us that Johnson's and Guthrie's care had done the real job. We hoped to see them again and were able to arrange some cables to their relatives. A football match was arranged between us and the crew of the *Celtic Star*, followed by a fraternal party given for us by Captain Mackie and his officers at the lodgings where they were accommodated. Then we were off to sea again with a small convoy to the French ports of Dakar and Conakry.

While we waited at Conakry for our return convoy, we got sudden orders to proceed to Freetown forthwith. "This looks like our marching orders," I said as we ploughed south. "Maybe there's a convoy southbound for the Cape, and we've got to join it." Our mood as we entered Freetown was one of detached resignation. Our first arrival there, the getting of our accumulated mail, and the sense of being in touch with our world again had all worked a helpful change.

News from home had been like rain after drought, slaking a desert. On the other hand it had sharpened memories and wakened desires and longings which absence had long drugged and sedated. Now if we were to set off southward for yet another stage of our interminable banishment, a sense of fatalism would inevitably set in again. We would make the best of it, enjoy some things, no doubt, certainly do our job as best we could. But it would be a struggle. It would be harder than before.

When the Captain stepped aboard after his visit to the Base Ship, I was waiting, as so often before, to hear the worst. Iceland, Halifax, New York, Bermuda, Trinidad, Brazil: the scene had been enacted against so many backgrounds, through such a catalogue of disappointments. This time the answer was different.

"We're going home."

In his cabin the Captain crammed his pipe with nervous fingers, spilling tobacco on the deck in his eagerness to tell me the story.

"We're paying off, here — probably after one more trip. I may have to go first — re-commissioning — new bunch coming out from the UK to take over."

I listened in a daze. Now at last the news we had waited to hear for nearly two years was reality; and for the moment I was numb, devoid of feeling. But as the strangeness wore off, warm currents of thankfulness began to course through me, a sense of well-being underlying every thought and action from that moment onwards.

The story was simple. Months before, while in Trinidad, the Captain and George had written to the Admiralty stating our case. *Buttermere* and *Wastwater* had been continuously on foreign service ever since the Norwegian campaign. A proportion of the ships' companies had been in them since commissioning at the beginning of the war. Our latest length of foreign service was detailed, with the difficult circumstances of our continually changing Administrative Authorities. In the opinion of the two Commanding Officers, morale was bound to decline.

On these grounds a request was made for re-commissioning if and when possible. The letters were two small voices crying in the wilderness; they were like bread cast upon water. Having despatched them in the appropriate form we had put the matter out of our minds. Certainly we had never expected any response, even a bare "Not Approved", before we reached South Africa. And now the answer had come, a generous complete answer. Our cry had been heard on high.

The "buzz" could not be contained; soon the whole ship knew of it. We were going home. Reliefs would be sent for us, officers and men. *Wastwater* and *Buttermere* were to pay off and recommission at Freetown. For us it would be a passage back to Britain, and foreign-service leave for sure! At long unbelievable last we were going home.

Among all the flowering of private hopes and plans, all the preparation and excitement, all the calculations and forecasts, all the unreliable buzzes of how and when, all the questions and counter-questions, there was a new spirit. The idea that we were meaningless cogs in a great impersonal machine was finally cancelled. Admiralty, that august Power at whose supreme behest we had scurried to and fro across the oceans; Admiralty, whose omnipotent Boot (as it sometimes seemed) had kicked us like a football all round the Atlantic, had heard our plea and in the final count had acted handsomely. It was a proof to us all — trawlermen, clerks, students or tramdrivers — that somewhere in the dusty precincts of Whitehall a human heart existed: that there were chaps, blokes, bastards (according to your choice of language) who were not deaf, and who would do their best for us if they could.

The Captain left in haste. A signal had come that he was urgently required at home "for a more important command". The turn of phrase caused some indignation on board.

"That can't mean anything less than a battleship," said Rattenbury.

The Captain went — passage in a destroyer — his bags hurled after him as the boat moved off from the gangway of the Base Ship, where *Wastwater* was lying alongside. "Good luck," a handshake, and the boat was off. He looked back, rather worried (where was that tricycle? had anything been forgotten?) and waved once. Then the boat disappeared round the bow and we saw him no more.

For a few days I was Acting CO. Then I was shaking hands with a smiling bearded officer on the deck of the Base Ship, and saying, as if in a dream, "Commanding Officer of *Wastwater*? I'm glad to see you. Had a good trip out?"

The days that followed would have been strenuous, quite apart from Freetown's exhausting climate. Paying off a ship is a hectic business at the best of times. In our case it was made more so by the complete turnover of the ship's company, officers and men. Our pay had to be made up to date — provisionally, as our pay accounts from the USA had not yet caught up with us. Messing accounts for the ship had to be settled (details had followed from the various ports we had visited). All items of any importance in the ship had to be mustered: stocks of provisions, naval stores, gunnery equipment, charts, instruments, and all Confidential

205

Books, which I went through individually with the new Commanding Officer.

"It's a nice cabin," I was able to assure him, "provided you are fond of cockroaches". In the Freetown heat, all our prodigious efforts with the Flit guns had been unable to stop their increasing multitude. At the same time Chief was taking the new Chief round the engine room, Bennet was showing the Asdic gear and stores to his relief, the Bunts and Sparks were turning over their equipment, in the galley the cooks (incoming and outgoing) were deep in culinary converse; while in the sweltering wardroom the new First Lieutenant sat struggling with the Watch and Quarter Bill for the new ship's company, still no more than names to him.

For both sides it was a trying process. *Wastwater* had been our home for so long, we knew her peculiarities so well, that it took a stretch of the imagination to understand the difficulties of newcomers. They, on their side, underestimated the difficulties of the Freetown climate, and the amount of sea time we had put in. Just as everything seemed clear, some new problem would crop up: where was this key kept, how was this bell wired? What were the local orders on this point? At last everything possible was mustered, signed and settled. We had done our best.

"As for the crew, you seem to have a pretty good bunch," I remarked to the new CO.

"Yes, they seem a good keen crowd. They'll soon shake down."

"She's a good ship. You get a bit attached to 'em after a while. Handles well, doesn't she?"

"Handles beautifully. I found that going up to the oiler this morning."

"Well, that seems about all, eh?"

"Yes, I think so, thanks very much."

A last look round together.

"This the Captain's shower? Not working? We'll get that fixed tomorrow."

My silence was, I believe, pregnant. But I deemed it best to let events take their course, so I merely said,

"Well, cheer-o, and best of luck."

"Best of luck to you too; thanks for everything."

We shook hands, I stepped out over the side and climbed the gangway to the deck of the Base Ship, high above. My gear had gone aboard that morning; Wilson, Rattenbury and all our old crew were there, waiting for passage. They had moved across a few days before. Half an hour later the new bunch were stowing their gear in *Wastwater*'s messdecks. She was ours no longer.

At five minutes to nine of the already languid morning, we stood on the deck of the Base Ship in Freetown waiting for the boat which would take us to the Armed Merchant Cruiser which in its turn would take us to Britain. We looked down for the last time on the deck of *Wastwater*, lying there alongside. Same ship, new ship's company. In the turmoil of paying off and turning over to our reliefs, there had been little time for sentimental reflection and in any case, when we did stop to think, the dominant fact that we were going home suffused the whole horizon with a cheerful light. *Wastwater* had been our home for nearly two years: a good deal more for some. But our affection did not make us wish to stay. We had been away together long enough. It was fitting and timely that we should go, that King Arthur's Table should be dispersed.

But now, looking down on those well-known decks for the last time, with nothing to do but wait for the boat to take us off, a strange weakness affected me, as I think some others. There was the round bow in which I had stood so often in the Icelandic blizzard or the burning tropical sun. There was the gun platform, with the new Gunner spilling oil in exactly the same spot as he cleaned the gun; the lookout bridge where I had chatted with the Bunts while we watched the floating dock on its way to St Thomas and from which the Captain had spotted the boats of the *Celtic Star*; the bridge itself where I had kept so many watches, and the congested boat-deck over which I had groped my way so often in the dead of night when called from my cabin aft. Every commonplace item was so full of meaning and association for us, so matter-of-fact to the newcomers. Would they ever quite understand?

Chief, leaning on the rail, shook his head wryly. His intimate knowledge of *Wastwater*'s mechanical foibles had impressed the Base Ship people, and invested him with a kind of aura. Well, old Chief, messenger of disaster, target of ribald comment which his gloomy aspect seemed to invite, and which his philosophic nature never resented, had the last laugh. Over a year and eight months, despite alarms and minor hold-ups, he had got us over thousands of miles of ocean, in all weathers, almost to a complete circumnavigation of the Atlantic.

He had his doubts about the new engine-room staff.

"Ah, them's been in coal-burnin' trawlers mostly. Oil's different — more tricky, like."

Guns, watching his successor at work, murmured, "They won't believe us when we tell 'em all the places we've been to."

More charitable critics judged the new crew "a good lot — but things have changed".

Surprisingly it was Old Bunts (he must have been at least twenty-one) who spoke loudest: Bunts, who had always been the stoutest champion of popular rights, the most articulate protester against arbitrary rule in the ship's routine, or in the wider world. The Left Book Club and satire against "Colonel Blimp" had stimulated his thinking. In talks on the bridge he had given me the clearest sense of the groundswell of discontent, the demand for a fairer society in Britain, which brought in the Attlee Labour government in 1945. His restless mind looked for something more than two fingers held up in a "V for Victory" sign. But now the argumentative, conversational Bunts had only one thing to say:

"There'll never be another ship like the *Wastwater*."

But even our last glimpse of *Wastwater* was not allowed to escape that element of comedy which had pursued her across years and oceans. As we watched, a rotund figure emerged on the casing and began work with a spanner on the after bulkhead of the bridge structure. It was the new Chief Engineman starting work on the Captain's shower.

CHAPTER 27

GOING HOME

The Armed Merchant Cruiser had been a luxury liner, running cruises to South America in peace-time. We marvelled at her immensity, her length and height, the great snowy white deck where *Wastwater* might almost have been accommodated as a lifeboat. Wilson, Rattenbury and I shared a sumptuous cabin with tasteful private bathroom attached. The dining saloon resembled a college hall, the state-room (now wardroom) was furnished with the elegance of a boudoir, the cinema on B Deck was spacious, the deck of the Boats Store consisted of ornamental rubber flooring, and in a corner stood the tables and fripperies of the dismantled Winter Garden.

Our lads were accommodated in some remote part of Leviathan. Occasionally we saw some of them, as at Boat Drill or sweeping (not too violently) one of the long passageways.

They had little to do, we had nothing. That was the most extraordinary sensation of all: to sit down in quiet privacy to read a book or write a letter, with the knowledge that no immediate urgent interruption was likely, took some getting used to. It was eerie that no Alf should rouse me in my cabin with the news "Wires parted fore and aft, Sir", no crescendo of ribald voices be wafted from a nearby galley.

Talking to officers of the AMC we wondered at the amenities of their life: the roomy cabins, well-appointed meals, easy watches, their smooth if monotonous routine. There, however, our envy stopped. Our lads, surveying the expanses of paintwork, the washing of which occupied much of the time of the AMC's deck crew, felt no hankering for big ship life. "You get lost aboard 'ere, Sir," said Alf. "Don't know which way you're facing."

A fisherman from boyhood, Alf had never been aboard a big ship in his life. As the great ship trundled on, Rattenbury and I would pace up and down the boat deck by the hour, or lean on the rail and look down from that immense height on the sparkling sea. The AMC was making better speed than *Wastwater* ever had, but the sensation of movement was far less.

Wastwater had always beaten the sea because, like a good swimmer, she had yielded herself so completely to it. "All the same," Rattenbury confided, "I thought we were gone once or twice in that ten days' gale off Nova Scotia."

Wilson joined our discussions from time to time, but he had discovered some New Zealand airmen among the passengers, and was usually hailed away to join some cheerful party or gregarious activity.

After two days of complete relaxation and luxurious idling a restlessness attacked me. I realised that this was an opportunity for evaluation such as might not come again, and the days were slipping by. In the year and eight months since we had sailed *Wastwater* out of Aberdeen we had accomplished an almost complete circuit of the North Atlantic: westwards to Iceland; north into the Arctic Circle; west again to Newfoundland, Canada, and the USA; south to St Thomas with the floating dock, and back to New York via the Caribbean and Key West; south-east again to Bermuda; from there northward to Nova Scotia, for our interlude with the cable ship; then south again in earnest to Bermuda, Trinidad and across the Line to Recife; from Recife to Freetown, re-crossing the Equator and the Atlantic; thence northward along the West African coast to Cape Verde and beyond. At every stage some eccentric providence seemed to have decreed for us the odd unusual job, taking us into ports and harbours rarely visited by what are termed "major" war vessels. As a mere catalogue of names it was a cruise such as few ships of our size and sort could have known in this war or any other.

Nor had we any need to be ashamed of our record. Throughout all that time we had been on foreign service, doing our full share of sea-time, on escort duty in submarine-haunted waters. We had not sunk a U-boat, but we had not lost a ship, and because we had been in the right place, sixty-three courageous men of the Merchant Navy had lived, not died, in mid-Atlantic. Our part along with others had been decisive in countering the U-boat threat on America's east coast.

Now, after leave, we would be going to new ships, new postings, we could not tell what. The tide of war seemed to be turning in favour of the Allies; but the struggle at sea against a resourceful, determined, reinforced enemy was far from over.

To me as an Australian, our voyage in *Wastwater* had brought insights into the varied inhabitants of the British Isles as no other experience could have done, and which were beyond price. Outstanding in my mind were their acceptance and enjoyment of one another's foibles, and their capacity to turn problems into entertainment. There had been trouble at times, there had been "non-cooperators", one or two, whom we had had to send ashore for disciplining. There had also been non-cooperators who had become cooperators. We remained free from those internal vendettas which can so easily wreck the life of any community. In all our twenty months of wandering, separated from our own folk and crowded together between narrow decks, I could not remember one serious quarrel. Some credit, no doubt, could be taken by us, the officers. But fundamentally it was something in the men themselves: a faculty for living together inherent in the British tradition, developed through centuries of struggle, setbacks and persistence.

Powerful factors reinforced morale and simplified decisions. The fervour of national commitment which underlay Britain's declaration of war against Germany, which I, like the vast majority of Britons, had wholeheartedly endorsed, had not weakened, but had developed into a world struggle not only for victory but for survival. By sea, land, and air, it was us or them, till the finish. The horror and cost of war had made many of us search deeper into basic realities than we had had to do in times of peace and security. An English Army friend serving in the Burma jungle had written:

> I have felt very English again after all these years of not bothering about my country — not Empire and dominion and all that, but for England's saving quality of tolerance tempering our arrogance. I feel the need of religion — not to

211

face death but to face life, to avoid losing the hope that the world will ever become wiser — for this kind of thing must not happen again.

An Australian school-friend, wounded in a Commando raid in Norway, wrote:

When one considers the wholesale ghastly agony of Europe, one realises that the individual right to happiness is absolutely cancelled.

He was killed later in Italy.

In *Wastwater* we had one special advantage. In a small ship — a microcosm of Britain — crossing oceans, visiting continents, our total interdependence was so obvious that it required no underlining, provided the need was clear. When a bungle (not ours) made it necessary, we had worked all night, officers and men, without a word of complaint, to get stores, ammunition and depth charges aboard before sailing at dawn. A war had to be won, we had a job to do. We would, literally, sink or swim together.

When had we been happiest: battling together for our lives in a Nova Scotian hurricane, or alongside in New York with distracting signals, defaulters and arguments about whose turn it was for leave?

I was grateful to have been received into the fellowship of seafarers: the Navy, where I had found much evidence of the humanity which Nelson had hoped would always be a characteristic of the British Fleet; but also others: the fishing trawler skippers in Iceland, the New York tug-boat captain, the cable ship officers, our friends from the *Celtic Star*.

What had Honor herself been learning? Her letters had been a life-line, so articulate and real and heartfelt. Yet the best of letters can only say so much. Probably they had been affected (as mine must have been also) by the nationwide stress on maintaining morale, on clinging to confidence and hope, on supporting the fighting men and women. Had there been other unspoken things? I longed to know; and now it would be possible. We were going home.

My heritage was two hemispheres. In *Wastwater* I had revisited the southern hemisphere and the night skies of the Southern Cross under which I was born. Now I could watch once more the climbing Pole Star, by which seafarers had calculated their latitude for centuries before the chronometer made possible the accurate reckoning of longitude. I thought of a poem:

Stella Polaris: Homebound

Above the great ship's lifting bow
I watch the Pole Star nightly stand,
nightly climbing clearer, higher;
ancient friend to sailors, now
lead to that remembered land
the end of all my heart's desire.

How often from my own small ship
I caught you in my sextant glass,
in those long months when hope must lie
in chrysalis, and I watched you slip
downward, and out of vision pass,
and the Southern Cross went up the sky —

those timeless months when time would slide
from watch to watch, from night to day
to night; when every thought must be
the moment's, lest, too fiercely eyed,
our tenuous hope dissolve away
and leave us with the endless sea.

And now (these dwindling leagues remaining
between me and my soul's delight)
fear fades, I grasp the promise given
as, scarce the turbulent joy refraining,

213

I stand with dumb full heart tonight
to watch the Pole Star climbing heaven.

The days became noticeably cooler. Whites were soon chilly
in the evenings. The fifth day we shifted to blue uniforms. How
strange and dowdy blue caps looked after white covers! Evenings
became longer, with a lingering twilight. It was the reverse process
of our southward dash from Halifax to Bermuda. During the last
few days of the trip, I was attacked by spasms of fear lest we
should be torpedoed: a reasonless dread that the circle of our
voyage, so nearly complete, would be maliciously broken in its
final stage. "Just what would happen," we said jocularly, as a
preventative incantation.

I had another apprehension. In those twenty months away I
had perfected a bunk technique, bracing my back against the bunk-
board, and my knee against the bulkhead opposite, which kept me
fixed and immovable. Through *Wastwater*'s wildest rolling I could
sleep tranquilly and undisturbed. But now: a bed without sides,
shared with another person? How wonderful: but how strange!
How would it be?

Then at tea someone said, "There's land in sight".

From the boat-deck I could see it clearly, faint and far in the
late afternoon sun, the rocky magnificent north coast of Ireland,
and there indeed were the comb-like teeth of Inishtrahull! We
were coming in through the Western Approaches of Britain, where
I had first met the grey swell of the North Atlantic, westbound
with those early ragged gallant convoys.

The ship had reduced speed, loitering so as not to arrive
before time. I slept a little. Wilson was talkative, Rattenbury quiet.
We packed and repacked several times, exchanged addresses and
plans. In the early morning when I went on deck we were in the
Clyde. I knew it all so well, those landlocked waters where I had
first ventured afloat as a professional sailor, with more misgivings
than I had since felt on ocean passages.

Astern was the friendly bird-whitened cone of Ailsa Craig; to
port, jagged blue and unforgotten, the mountains of Arran; to

starboard, the Ayrshire coast; beyond that Dumfries, where our Robert was buried; and away further, in the dawn light, all the island of Britain, with my wife and son Peter.

In the bustle of preparation, I glimpsed Alf, Chief and some of the others, wished them "All the best" and heard their chorused "Same to you, Sir."

When the Customs Officials and the Sea Transport Officer had come aboard and made all necessary arrangements for us, we went down to the waiting drifter, crossed the deep-water anchorage, and landed on Gourock Pier.